Brainball

Brainball

Teaching Inquiry Theater as a Team Sport

Mickey Kolis, Benjamin H. Kolis,
and
Tara Lorence

ROWMAN & LITTLEFIELD
Lanham • Boulder • New York • London

Published by Rowman & Littlefield
A wholly owned subsidiary of The Rowman & Littlefield Publishing Group, Inc.
4501 Forbes Boulevard, Suite 200, Lanham, Maryland 20706
www.rowman.com

Unit A, Whitacre Mews, 26-34 Stannary Street, London SE11 4AB

Copyright © 2017 by Mickey Kolis, Benjamin H. Kolis, and Tara Lorence

All rights reserved. No part of this book may be reproduced in any form or by any electronic or mechanical means, including information storage and retrieval systems, without written permission from the publisher, except by a reviewer who may quote passages in a review.

British Library Cataloguing in Publication Information Available

Library of Congress Cataloging-in-Publication Data Available

ISBN: 978-1-4758-3469-7 (cloth : alk. paper)
ISBN: 978-1-4758-3470-3 (pbk. : alk. paper)
ISBN: 978-1-4758-3471-0 (electronic)

∞™ The paper used in this publication meets the minimum requirements of American National Standard for Information Sciences—Permanence of Paper for Printed Library Materials, ANSI/NISO Z39.48-1992.

Printed in the United States of America

Contents

Foreword	ix
Acknowledgments	xi
Introduction	xiii

SECTION ONE: BRAINBALL (THEATER EDITION): WHY THEATER MATTERS   **1**

1. Brainball (Theater Edition): The Point of the Game Is Learning   5
2. The Big Ideas: Product, Process, and Community Aligned with Purpose   13
3. Brainball (TE): Beliefs (Dispositions)   19
4. Brainball (TE): Key Concepts (Knowledge)   29
5. Brainball (TE): Skills   37

SECTION TWO: PREPARING TO COACH THE GAME   **41**

6. Tip 1: Keep the End in Mind   43
7. Tip 2: Play the Game   53
8. Tip 3: Competitions as Evaluations   59
9. Tip 4: Sequences Matter   63
10. Tip 5: Explicit Communications   75

SECTION THREE: DAY-TO-DAY LESSON PLANS: BRAINBALL ILLUMINATED — 81

11 Lesson Plans — 85
    Lesson 1: Observations: Fitting In — 85
    Lesson 2: Observations: Learning to Be More Observant — 87
    Lesson 3: Observations: Guided Theater — 88
    Lesson 4: Curiosity: I Wonder Statements — 91
    Lesson 5: Problem Statements — 93
    Lesson 6: Gathering Information: Voice — 94
    Lesson 7: Gathering Information: Space — 96
    Lesson 8: Gathering Information: Writing Scripts — 98
    Lesson 9: Gathering Information: Costumes — 99
    Lesson 10: Gathering Information: Set Design — 100
    Lesson 11: Gathering Information: Feedback and Feedforward — 102
    Lesson 12: Create: Pick and Plan — 103
    Lesson 13: Create: Compose — 105
    Lesson 14: Create: Compose — 106
    Lesson 15: Create: Review and Revise — 107
    Lesson 16: Create: Review — 108
    Lesson 17: Create: Revise — 109
    Lesson 18: Create: Construct — 110
    Lesson 19: Create: Test — 111
    Lesson 20: Create: Test — 112
    Lesson 21A: Perform: (In-Class) — 113
    Lesson 21B: Evening Performance—Showcase Event — 114
    Lesson 22: Analysis of the Entire Inquiry Process — 114
    Lesson 23: Conclusion: What Have We Learned? — 115

Conclusion — 117

Appendices
    Appendix 1: Steps of Theater Inquiry — 119
    Appendix 2: SCAMPER — 123
    Appendix 3: Getting the Most from Experiences — 125
    Appendix 4: Cross the Line Prompts — 131
    Appendix 5: Circle of Power and Respect (CPR) — 133
    Appendix 6: Sample Script — 135
    Appendix 7: Stage Directions — 137

Appendix 8: Blocking Activity	139
Appendix 9: Script Writing	141
Appendix 10: Set Rendering	143
Appendix 11: Scoring Guide	145
Appendix 12: Story Arc	147
Appendix 13: Script Template	149
Appendix 14: Feedback Form	151
Appendix 15: Costume Worksheet	153
Appendix 16: Set Design Worksheet	155
Appendix 17: Set and Costume Planning Worksheet	157
Appendix 18: Performance Reflection Worksheet	159
References	161

Foreword

In English, the word *play* is employed to designate dramatic texts and performance events. Contained in the idea of *play* as an object ("I watch a *play*") and a space ("I'm in a *play*") is the ludic nature of performance itself. *Brainball* (TE) considers theater (*play*) not just as a field/object of study, but most importantly, as a tool to facilitate teaching and learning.

    Through a series of superbly organized, structured, guided exercises, and lesson plans Lorence proposes an alternative way of teaching and making theater in the classroom. *Brainball* (TE) proposes a change in how the traditional theater classroom engages with the creative process of making performance by placing equal value on production, development, and community—reinforcing the power of process and collaboration as learning and teaching tools.

    In addition, Kolis and Kolis have devised a methodological paradigm in *Brainball* (TE) that consistently engages with an inclusive, self-reflexive practice rooted in creativity and the potential of embodied ways of learning that, in turn, invite us to consider how the skills acquired by students while learning through and about theater have the potential to transfer to other occupations and learning endeavors. Ultimately, *Brainball* (TE) posits theater as conduit to learn about self and the world around us.

Henry MacCarthy
Gustavus Adolphus College
St. Peter, MN

Acknowledgments

I'd like to acknowledge my family and friends for their constant encouragement and support throughout my educational career. I'd also like to thank my middle school students at Columbia Academy in Columbia Heights, MN, for teaching me that no substantial learning can occur without a substantial relationship.

—Tara Lorence

Because of my work as an actor and director, *Brainball* (Theater Edition [TE]) is a project near and dear to my heart. Thanks to Amy Seham, Henry MacCarthy, and Rebecca Fremo who helped educate me despite all my efforts to the contrary. Thanks to cocreator Tara Lorence, whose super-structured lesson plans make up the meat of this book, and who inspired me to be a little more structured in my own thinking. Thanks to my endlessly loving and forgiving mother, Jeanne Kolis, and thanks to my long-suffering and incredibly patient partner Teige. Of course, thanks to cocreator/driving force/dad (figuratively for others but literally for me) Mickey Kolis. Without Mickey's ability to toggle between his green personality and his much more reluctant yellow personality, *Brainball* (TE) would have been lost.

—Benjamin H. Kolis

Sometimes in life, we get the opportunity to talk about topics that are important—really important. Letting students (and people generally) roleplay others gives them powerful experiences with seeing things from perspectives other than their own. To me (and the other authors) that is a foundational piece to growing empathy. Thanks to Tara and Ben for being my co-travelers on this journey! Collaborations can be trying—not with them! I would also like to thank (once again) my wonderful wife, Jeanne, and our sons who continuously help me see life from different perspectives.

—Mickey Kolis

Introduction

Games are powerful learning tools. Since *Brainball* (Theater Edition [TE]) is a game as well as a teaching methodology, it makes sense to spend a little bit of time clarifying what exactly games are.

So, what are games? One might think of card games, board games, athletics, and video/computer games. These are all games. All of them rely on different sets of rules and have different requirements of its players; some games are physical, some intellectual, social, or emotional. Some are for individuals, some for teams. Despite the variations, all games have several things in common.

1. Games are the transformation of theory and practice into performance. Games are activities. Activities, as in action. Games are meant to be played, the *doing* of theory. The rules are the theory, and the enacting of the rules is the playing of the game.
2. All games have a clear goal. If you don't know the end to a game that is played, there is no reason to play. For most games, the overarching goal is winning, which means accomplishing a specific goal as laid out in the rules (theory) of the game better, faster, or with more skill than the other players.
3. All games have a clear set of rules. The rules are the theory of the game. The limits and restrictions of a game is what defines the game itself—that is, soccer is defined by its specific rules regarding out-of-bounds, which players do what, and how a team scores. These rules make the game different than, say, basketball, or backgammon.
4. Chance is part of the game. Without chance, a game is math. The role of a dice, the bouncing of a ball, and human error are all ways that chance manifests itself in games.

5. Multiple strategies and skills can lead to success. Creativity is an advantage. Real games use the rules to inspire creativity rather than to crush it. Rules that inspire creativity are what give a game replay value. The best games are the most engaging, provide opportunities for multiple strategies to lead to success, and are interesting (physically, intellectually, socially, emotionally, or morally).
6. To be effective at the game, players need to be adaptable. Situations during games change, and players need to be able to use a strategy and change it on the fly.
7. People play games because they perceive them as fun. "Fun" is defined as "appropriately challenging." Too much challenge is discouraging and too little is boring. Think of a middle school basketball team competing against a high school basketball team: The middle schoolers would be discouraged, and the high schoolers would be bored. No one would be having fun.
8. Games are dynamic. The more a player knows, the less he knows. The more he knows, the more complex the game becomes, the more work he has to put in to become better. Playing the game itself makes it clear what players need to learn next to improve. Games provide immediate, concrete consequences for decisions players make.

A quick note about fun and the dynamic game: Fun is the point of a game, and with a group of players who understand this, the rules of a given game are fluid. Rules should make the game fun. Think of sand-lot baseball games; while the players may call it baseball, chances are good that the players of the game have a set of rules different than Major League Baseball (ghost runners, pitcher's hand, right field out, etc.). This is to make the game fun for them. This is dynamic and requires a complex understanding of how a game works.

One might notice that theater meets many of these same eight characteristics: There is a clear goal (expressing an experience through representative action), there are rules (theory), and success rests upon the ingenuity and determination of the players ("Well, what if X instead of Y?" "Let's give it a try").

Many people find theater to be fun in very personal, individualized ways. The big difference between theater in general and theater in a classroom is that students do not perceive the learning of theater as fun. They just want to be entertained.

Thespians act every day, yet when it comes to learning theater, it seems to be looked at as work. Students playing a role from a play know how to act, but do they really know how to *act* when they play?

Introduction xv

THEATER AS PLAY AND PLAY AS THEATER

Imagine for a moment a "typical" middle or high school theater classroom. Probably the class is either performance-based (grades are given depending on how well the students perform assigned material) or theory-based (grades are given depending on how well the students remember vocabulary and content).

A few star students answer all of the questions or are cast as leads immediately, while the bottom students fade into the background. Maybe no one ever learns some of their names. Students are either competing for roles (or trying to avoid being selected for roles) or competing to have their hands in the air first. In either case, the teacher/director is at the top of the pyramid with students underneath, waiting to be told what to do, how to learn their part to his satisfaction. What is "good" is what the director or teacher wants with no exception.

The only curiosity from the students in the classroom is wondering which play they will work on that day or if the teacher is going to finally pick a play, they want to learn. Class feels like a distraction from real life; there are more pressing and important things to be thinking about.

There is little connection in the theater to what students are learning in other classes, not to mention the topics students think about in the halls. Students focus on learning their lines exclusively for the performance, then they move on to the next play. It is difficult to imagine a theater classroom, or any performance-based classroom any other way.

The authors of this book have been in this class, or one like it (maybe we've even taught it before), and we imagine that you have as well. Frankly, it is irrelevant. It's not fun.

And a lot of what makes it irrelevant is structural; you have a group of people with various levels of commitment, with different skills, with different experiences, who may or may not like one another. That's tough—structurally and otherwise.

So what happens if we think about the structure in a different way? What if we thought about this class as a team, like a soccer or baseball team? What game would they be playing? Would it have replay value? Would it be "fun?"

And what would a "Theater Team" look like exactly (I don't know about you, but I don't recall a whole lot of crossover between my theater friends and my soccer friends in high school)? Would a Theater Team get the same benefits from "teamness" that a soccer team does?

Let's start with that: Teamness. There are lots of different teams, and all of them are organized around competition—the measurement of yourself or your team against something else. There are average teams, good teams, and then there are great teams.

Level 1: An Average Team

- Skills are taught and practiced in isolation
- Players (and the coaches) exhibit a consumerism mentality ("me" focus)
- The focus is on winning rather than learning
- The coaches make all the decisions
- Competition exists between players on the same team. Cliques are the norm
- Players and coaches look for ways to bend the rules, not get caught, and win at any cost
- The other team and the referee are perceived as the enemy

But that is only the first level. No coach would be satisfied with that. Good teams are characterized by:

Level 2: A Good Team

- There is an excellent focus on individual development
- The team as a community is implicit (or happens by random chance)
- Individuals understand their own role and those of a few others
- The team is built around one or two outstanding players
- Winning is the shared vision of the team
- There is at least a surface acknowledgment that many people have important roles
- The focus is to play the game well, and worse players are to support the better players

And at the highest level, great teams are characterized by:

Level 3: A Great Team

- There is alignment between individual learning and team learning goals
- There is an explicit community focus where everyone contributes to the whole group (and contributions are acknowledged and valued)
- Diversity is seen as a strength of the team (everyone plays a special role)
- People are committed to team vision (beyond compliant and enrolled)
- The team learning goal is clear and explicit (to play the game with integrity and rules make the game)
- The game has an external audience
- Support is appropriate (emotionally, socially, intellectually, morally, and physically)
- Knowledge, skills, and dispositions are integrated as part of the daily conversation

- The coach makes him/herself dispensable (decentralization of authority)
- Team members remember their shared experiences as powerful and important
- The team views competitions as learning events (they are one measure, not the goal)

One last characteristic of great teams is the potential to create something greater than the sum of its parts. Great teams leave the participants with positive lasting memories—they change people's lives. To be part of something unforgettable is worth thinking and dreaming about.

This however seems pretty translatable to me. Many of us can recall a theatrical project that had the elements of a great team—and maybe that's why we kept doing theater. Theater as a discipline *wants to* work as a team; theater *wants to* be played like a game.

While there are multiple ways to use this book, the intent is to build great teams with students. One way to use this book is to go through it sequentially. Section 1 provides the "Big Picture" of the game (the "why?" questions are answered there). Section 2 explains the most important ideas to keep in mind as a teacher preparing to coach *Brainball* (TE).

Some will undoubtedly start with section 3: the "How to" section (that works as well). Those daily lesson plans are formatted using a 5Es structure (see section 3), and the entire sequence shows how to teach the process of Theater Inquiry (see appendix 1). The lesson plans in section 3 have been designed and tested (multiple times) so time frames are close to reality (really!).

Brainball (TE) is an attempt to clarify that not only is theater a game but that it is one of the most useful and powerful games that teachers and students will ever play. Games are the *doing* of theory, and maybe it would be a good idea to start *doing* theater in every theater classroom.

Section One

BRAINBALL (THEATER EDITION)
Why Theater Matters

The purpose of theater is "the expression of the human experience through representative actions" (Kolis, 2011). That means we need to clarify "the human experience." The big ideas that make up the human experience include:

1. People—their needs (and how they go about meeting them), strengths and weaknesses; issues of race/class/gender/sexual orientation, and so on; developmental issues and changes; interests and hobbies; and the ability to deal with change (and that means risk).
2. Context—the place where things occur, the time things are happening, the knowledge of that time and place (the information, paradigms, and belief systems), the culture (what's valued, who's in charge, the rules and laws, etc.) and life, and national and world events that might be causing shifts to take place.
3. Conflict—intrapersonal (knowing self), interpersonal (relationships), cultural (between social and economic groups), and global (between large groups of people). These conflicts may be addressed through the use of force—conflict may also be in terms of ideas, philosophies, and/or economic struggles.
4. Power—how does one get it, keep it when they get it, and use it (for what purpose)? This also includes the idea of "enoughness"—how much is enough?
5. Resources—food, water, gold, clean air, diamonds, and so on. It always depends on what is limited and in demand at that time and place.

While these big ideas of the human experience are important to understand, what really matters is the individual experience—how each individual processes the things that are happening to them (it is all about ME!). Each of us processes our experiences in our own ways, through our unique combination of multiple intelligences, beliefs, and past experiences. Even if we are in the same place at the same time, we can each walk away with very different "experiences."

All of that means that theater is about expressing those experiences that make us human (as an individual)—it is our *story* in representative actions. Theater matters (when taught as doing theater rather than performance) because when the focus shifts from only a performance that expresses someone else's experience to studying my human experience (things that are students are most concerned about right now) it has the capacity to enhance everyone's quality of life.

And that means our study of theater needs to be question driven: Why do people do this? Why do I feel this way? How can I make other people understand? Asking discipline-specific questions (and then answering them) is called inquiry (appendix 2). When teaching theater inquiry, first you study the human experiences, THEN learn to express them through representative actions.

And it matters that we express them. Things we are unable or unwilling to express literally drive us crazy. We have these thoughts, experiences, and quandaries, and they are in us. We need to express them to get them out of our minds and look at them from another perspective. We need to find others who have shared or empathize with what matters to us *right now*.

Theater matters because words alone are slippery. We can say the same word, we both nod our heads in agreement, yet we miscommunicate because we each have our own definition of that term. And there are thoughts, ideas, and/or feelings that cannot be expressed adequately using only words.

Those two ideas (humanness and representative actions) blend together when we teach theater. Powerful theater instruction means studying the things that our students are struggling with (right now)—and then putting those concepts to representative actions. That means love, and belonging, and not fitting in, and the struggle for independence, and dating, and rejection, and celebrations, and joy and happiness, and oh, so much more that plays with their minds. It means all the things that make us human (in developmentally appropriate ways).

Theater allows us to speak in ways that other methods of communication cannot. Theater provides a personal, reflective opportunity to express what matters to us as human beings. It is like journaling (for those who process through text) or creating a piece of art (for those who process through two- or three-dimensional representations) or dancing by yourself (for those who process through movement)—it is how you process your reality (theater is the expression of *your* human experience). It represents your ideas of beauty, joy, sadness, failure, success, perseverance, resilience, conflict—all those things that make us human.

Brainball (TE) attempts to stress the making of theater versus only the performing of theater. A "performance-only" model misses the point entirely, just like teams that only focus on winning rather than learning. Brainball (TE) is process driven, not product driven.

Theater is a way of thinking and communicating. It differs from other disciplines in how those experiences are communicated. Plays are the communiques from people who have created representative actions to express their experiences. The play itself is *not* theater, nor is a set, a light, or any other piece of equipment. True theater happens in the mind and because of that it is ever changing. And that is the neatest thing about it.

Games are defined (*Merriam-Webster*, 2002) as a procedure or strategy for gaining an end (the end product of Brainball (TE) being "the expression of the human experience through representative actions in a community of learners").

The game of theater is dynamic and incorporates new facts versus old beliefs, the search for new perspectives and experiences and ways of thinking, and the realization that the more one knows the more one realizes there is more to know.

Theater—more than many other disciplines—is rooted in games. Lots of rehearsals begin with a sober, "Let's play," because it is at once incredibly fun and deadly serious to envision alternative realities. "Theater Games" are used in all sorts of contexts, from corporate get-to-know-you parties to community education classes to neighborhood meetings—we want to be theatrical when we're around people. It's part of being human.

But "being theatrical" and "doing theater" are difficult, which is why we so often limit ourselves to one-off games: It's easier to think about using the human experience—like being vulnerable, uncomfortable, afraid, or brave—as an accessory to a greater end, like employers hoping that a trust fall or an improving class will increase productivity, or even a theater teacher who hopes a name game will help his/her students perform a Shakespeare play.

Doing theater is harder than playing a few theater games. Doing theater means playing the game of theater, which (like any other really good game) takes more than a weekend retreat to learn.

Playing the game of theater well requires expertise in three different areas: knowledge (concepts, facts, and connections), skills (things one can do), and dispositions (tendency to act in certain ways under certain conditions) that are unique to the theater (every content area has its own unique combination).

Brainball (TE) is about people creating personal knowledge, developing their skills, and developing theater dispositions. Of the three, dispositions are the most important (especially for students) because they are the most personal and therefore the hardest things to change.

This is the first of several sections. Section 1 (these first five chapters) introduces the basics of Brainball (TE). Chapter 1 introduces the game of Brainball (TE) and chapter 2 clarifies the Big Ideas that drive its structure. Chapter 3 clarifies what the authors mean by theater beliefs, chapter 4 describes the Key Concepts required to play the game and chapter 5 introduces the skills needed to play the game.

So let's play.

Chapter One

Brainball (Theater Edition)
The Point of the Game Is Learning

BRAINBALL (TE) ENVISIONED

You have been invited into a seventh–eighth-grade middle school theater class, third quarter, which has been playing Brainball (TE) since day one of the school year. You decide to go since you've heard the kids talking about the class and you're curious. Today is the day.

You walk in before the bell, being greeted at the door with a high-five by one of the students, see the kids getting their stuff out for class, and hear them talking about what they have to accomplish for the day. You think, "This is kind of unusual."

The teacher and students greet you and get started as the bell rings. The teacher points to the learning goal for the day and shows a clip from movie—one of the characters is clearly in charge of the situation. The teacher breaks them into groups to come up with "3 ways to show a power relationship."

After a few minutes, the teacher asks each group to show their two best representations. After each short bit, the class records what was effective and what wasn't. The teacher uses their answers as a jumping-off point for the "lecture." The teacher clarifies ideas, adds information, and references their answers. Students are totally engaged with the process and suggest other situations and performances as examples.

After five minutes, the teacher calls a stop to the dialogue and students get into their "theater teams" and use the information they've just talked about to rework scenes/sections from the pieces they've been making. Students are in teams of threes or fours.

It's clear that each group has begun to stage their own short pieces. They seem to be thematically centered on the concept of "power." The groups are improvising through scenes, writing down text and stage directions, and performing short snippets for one another; they are laughing and making mistakes, but obviously getting work done.

The groups seem to be flexible. You notice students asking questions and advice from other groups. There seem to be classroom "experts." You notice students are asking other groups to critique their work. They take these critiques seriously but not personally. It's clear that everyone knows everyone by name.

Surprisingly, a group approaches you and asks if you'd watch a section of their piece. They're going to be using a prop and want to see if it works. As you watch, you notice that they are confident in their work, even though their scene obviously needs more work. They ask challenging questions about their work and appreciate your honesty.

With 15 minutes left, the groups put everything away and arrange a performance space in the front of the room. The teacher asks each group to perform a section of their pieces dealing with power or to discuss the changes they plan to make. Students give critiques and ask questions about the work, and the teacher connects the answers and performances to the learning goal of the day.

As the class ends, you think about the key ideas you've noticed: (a) Students were talking to one another like professionals (their language was content rich and appropriate), (b) they seemed to know that what they did yesterday mattered today and were aware of what was going to be taking place tomorrow, and (c) all of the students seemed to have a valuable role in their groups and the classroom.

The last thing that struck you as unique was that the students seemed to have a really good time in class (like it was "fun")—and they in fact learned something.

LEARNING

The point of Brainball (TE) is to offer an alternative method for how to think about teaching theater. Brainball (TE) is about having students actively create and reflect upon theater—to *play* the game of theater. Though you might consider a Venn diagram of "actors" and "athletes" to have a small intersection, the vocabulary and spirit of popular athletics is directly applicable to the game of theater and suggests simple but important ways that we can make theater more relevant to our students—Brainball: The Sport of Theater!

Brainball (TE) is a game focused on student learning (rather than only performing); learning being defined as "a change in thoughts, beliefs and actions" (*Merriam-Webster*, 2002). This means that the individuals themselves choose when and what they have "learned." A focus on student learning is different from the performance-driven model currently used in many theater classrooms.

"Learning" means that the individual has to and/or gets to decide what it is about themselves that they are changing—and that is a high-risk activity. Playing the game as a team reduces the risk for all players involved. Great Teams (see the Introduction) provide a sense of belonging, working together to create something worthwhile, synergy, a "work from strengths" perspective, and appropriate intellectual, emotional, social, physical, and moral support.

"Learning" means change, and change (for everyone) is difficult—change doesn't guarantee a more fulfilling future. Change is scary. Change is high risk, with no guarantee of success. It is easy to forget that the job of educators is to help people grow and change (for the better hopefully).

Some people fear change because they believe that everything has to change at the same time. In reality, if dispositions were the focus of education, small changes can do enormous amounts of work. One small change leads to another and another—and before you know it, life looks different.

This cumulative process of learning can be uncomfortable, but adaptation is the most powerful of all human traits. The learning journey is so basic, that many, if not all, enduring human stories are variations of that single theme.

In the book *The Hero's Journey*, Brown and Moffett look at the similarities between some of these learning stories, including *The Chronicles of Narnia*, *The Lord of the Rings*, and *Hamlet*. They divided learning journeys into the following stages:

1. Innocence lost
2. Chaos and complexity
3. The heroic quest
4. Gurus and alliances
5. Trials, tests, and initiations
6. Insight and transformations

For example, *The Lord of the Rings* follows the main character, Frodo. Before Frodo begins his journey, he is comfortably living in his hobbit hole. He comes into the possession of the One Ring (innocence lost), which propels him across the world of Middle Earth (chaos and complexity). To resolve the chaos, he learns that the One Ring must be destroyed (the heroic quest), and he and the Fellowship of the Ring set out to do so (gurus and alliances). One by one, they are separated, leaving Frodo and Sam by themselves to struggle on toward the slopes of Mt. Doom (trials, tests, and initiations). They destroy the One Ring and return to the Shire as changed halflings (insight and transformation).

The *Harry Potter* series perhaps speaks a similar story to a different generation. The saga of the Boy Who Lived is another perfect example of the *Hero's Journey*. His innocence lost, the chaos, the goal, the friends and advisors, the trials, and the ultimate transformation follow the pattern set forth in the *Hero's Journey* perfectly, both within each book and as a series.

Literary journeys are made even more powerful because the dispositions of the characters play a vital and explicit role. What is the trait that allows Harry to succeed against all odds? As Dumbledore tells Harry again and again—love. In the *Harry Potter* saga, love is the disposition that holds everything together. It is the characters' deep understanding of a simple principle (love) that gives them insight into everything—maybe not the finer points, but certainly the basics.

Though it might seem a stretch to compare an epic like *The Lord of the Rings* or *Harry Potter* to a seventh- or eighth-grade theater classroom, the *Hero's Journey* models the learning journeys, both large and small, equally well.

LEARNING IN TEAMS

The *Hero's Journey* is one way to consider the learning process of individuals. Since each human creates his own knowledge, the importance of the individual experience is seminal. Brainball (TE) is a team sport; however, one must acknowledge the team as well as the individual learning journey.

Learning happens socially as well as individually. Communities of learners help and support each other as each person undertakes their own Hero's Journey. But to do so effectively, each group takes on a collective Hero's Journey. Because of the connection between the collective and individual experience, classroom communities need to be structured in a way that fosters support and credits the individual experience.

The classroom experience needs to be rooted in contributions rather than consumerism. If a classroom inhibits the already difficult and uncomfortable individual learning journey, students will find other ways to meet their needs. Structuring a supportive community is difficult, but possible.

Communities have their own version of the stages of an individual's Hero's Journey. In his book *Five Dysfunctions of a Team*, Patrick Lencioni discusses the community version of the *Hero's Journey*. Community learning steps address the following:

1. Absence of trust
2. Fear of conflict
3. Lack of commitment

4. Avoidance of accountability
5. Inattention to results

Think about the movie *Remember the Titans*. It is the story of a newly integrated high school football team in Virginia in the early 1970s. Though the team begins with many of these five dysfunctions, the Titans suffer largely a lack of trust in their teammates, primarily between the white and African American players on the team. The five dysfunctions are an excellent method to categorize and address problems in a community.

Our culture is rich with stories about the transformation of a community, especially ones that deal with athletics. Think of some of the really enduring sports movies: *Miracle on Ice*, *Remember the Titans*; even *Cool Runnings* and *The Mighty Ducks* are all examples of groups of individuals that overcame some or all of the five dysfunctions and learned how to work together as a community.

Unlike the *Hero's Journey*, the five dysfunctions don't take place in a sequence, but rather can happen at any time in any sequence; the dysfunctions must be addressed as they arise. Neither does a community have to experience all of the five dysfunctions equally; maybe a group has more of a problem with trust than fear of conflict.

The dysfunctions that a team struggles with is a reflection of the dispositions that the group values. When a team has overcome a dysfunction (such as when the Titans begin to see themselves as a team [community] with black and white players, rather than white and black players on the same team), it means the team has changed the dispositions it values.

A team that is able to overcome the five dysfunctions of a team is a community that will foster learning and credit the individual learning journey as not only important but also vital to the success of the group.

THE POINT OF THE GAME

Winning may be an extrinsic indicator of many games, but in Brainball (TE) winning is just one indicator of how well the players understand and act creatively within the rules of the game. The end-in-mind in Brainball (TE) is learning—for the students and the instructor.

Making explicit that learning is the end-in-mind of the game matters because in athletics, winning a competition against another team is overstressed. The win–loss of a team record directly measures success or failure of the entire season. With this focus, learning takes a peripheral position.

In theater classes, performing for a wider audience is common (unlike many other classes), but the focus is often solely on play selection and an evaluation (how well did they perform?). Rarely is the focus on the process of learning and on the content learned within the learning process. To look at it another way, rarely is the focus on something outside of just "winning" (i.e., performing the play really well).

The game of Brainball (TE) is exploring the many ways to express the human experience through representative actions in a community of learners. The active form is *how well* students ask questions and pursue these expressions in a community of learners. *Doing* theater is Brainball (TE). Doing theater, unlike doing soccer, is not an athletic endeavor, but an intellectual game, a mind game.

Communities are based on individuals making contributions to the whole, which is the opposite of consumerism. A community relies on every person contributing something to the good of the group. A true community knows that their overall strength lies in a diversity of strengths. Powerful communities also have decentralized authority—everyone is both leader and follower.

Picture a soccer team: Though there's a coach on the sideline, it's the players on the field making decisions, and though the coach may later disagree, everyone on the team understands that the individual makes the best decision he could at that time, knowing what he knew—any judgment passed after the fact is a learning opportunity. Each player on the field is the expert of his or her position, and each position is important.

When the ball is played to the sweeper, the striker knows that right now, the responsibility is on the person best suited to handle it, and knows that when they themselves receives the ball, their teammates know the same of them and move to support them. The player with the ball has the power to decide the next play.

Now imagine a theater classroom playing Brainball (TE): Though there is a teacher (director), the players in the room are making theatrical decisions that they think are right at that time and place. Each player is working in their area of strength and everyone is important so that the whole can succeed (learn).

Responsibility lies upon the person best suited to handle it, and everyone knows that their turn to contribute will happen soon. The player who needs to make the immediate decision has the power to decide the next step.

Learning is an experience that changes the way a person thinks, acts, or believes. Memorization is not necessarily learning, and a performance does not necessarily measure learning. Learning changes the way one's mind works. People make decisions the best they can knowing what they knew at the time—learning is when people make different decisions.

RELEVANCE

When a student asks, "Why do we have to perform this play?" and the only answer he gets is "because audiences love this play," or "it's a classic," the student instinctively knows that the teacher does not possess a deep understanding of the topic (or the students). Why should they spend time learning plays they will never perform again and that the teacher himself cannot justify knowing?

Eating and sleeping increase the quality of life. What does theater do? Students know that theater is important in a far-off and abstract way. Theatrical learning isn't relevant to them because teachers don't demonstrate that it can make their lives better. But theatrical learning *is* relevant. And it *does* increase the quality of life. Teachers just have to teach it that way.

Teachers can be an expert in their content area and still be poor teachers. Many teachers (directors) understand content and hope that students will care enough on their own to actually learn (change), that they will see that the presented selection is somehow *relevant*. They hope that the students will see the human connection.

This is an ineffective model. If a teacher makes teaching the plays rather than teaching the students the focus of their lessons, then they themselves do not believe that the information is relevant. If a teacher merely presents plays, if they are not capable of using the information they present to improve their own life, they are not teaching people but rather reading a script. Their information is irrelevant.

Relevance means that people do something because they want to—they believe that that thought, that action, or that belief will best meet their needs. When something is relevant, people spend their time, effort, and resources on that task/activity/game. They see it as "fun."

This is true for hobbies, sports, crafts, and other enjoyable activities (fishing, cooking, sewing, soccer, etc.). People spend money, time, and effort participating, planning, learning, and *doing* the things they enjoy. No one makes them do it—it is their choice!

Students have questions—about themselves, others, their role in the world, right and wrong, fitting in, and oh so many more. Most of the time they are left to fend for themselves as they create answers. Theater provides a space to study that human experience, to ponder alternatives, to wonder who and how else.

Theater is relevant when it teaches people how to effectively express the human experience through representative actions, and is especially relevant when it teaches people how to be contributing members in learning communities. "Express" in this case does not just mean perform by playing an instrument or singing; it is referring to the variety of ways that theater can be best expressed for an individual, through means such as composing, set design, performing, researching, and analyzing.

When things are "relevant" (meaningful to the individual) the individual believes that the "new" thought, belief, or action will meet his needs more effectively than what he is currently thinking, doing, or believing. Relevance means they are willing to give their time, effort, and resources to "learn" something. It may more fully meet their need for power, fun, freedom, or love and belonging (human needs).

If they in fact "play the game" they will in reality "enhance their quality of life" because they will learn about themselves, how to deal with change, deal with challenges, learn to support others, notice and solve problems, express their experiences through actions, share power, and celebrate hard-won victories.

To be clear, Brainball (TE) isn't about college. College professors are not required to be good teachers (though it never hurts), they are required to be content experts. The assumption goes that by the time students get to college, they should possess the motivation and skills to take information and make it relevant without the help of a teacher—and most are.

Brainball (TE) is a dynamic enterprise (like any game with staying power) because things are always in flux. Players need to have the skills, the knowledge, and the dispositions to deal with the ever-changing nature of every game (life). No matter how well prepared you feel, the game itself requires a flexibility of thought, strategy, and choices—that is what makes them "fun" (appropriately challenging) and stressful at the same time.

Brainball (TE) is one way of viewing the teaching and learning world. It attempts to use the strengths of two apparently disparate activities to create an alternative vision for learning in a theater setting. The real competition is within the individual/team, not against the other team. Competition's role is to help students and teams find out what they need to "learn" next to better meet their ever-evolving needs.

Chapter Two

The Big Ideas

Product, Process, and Community Aligned with Purpose

Society loves products. Many citizens love feeling that their lives are packaged into neat little pieces, easy to consider and understand. This is especially true with how schools and learning are currently structured. In today's world, and especially in education, everything "important" has to be measured (quantified) and evaluated. Without some kind of comparison, it would be difficult to decide what is successful and what isn't, where to allocate funding, who to hire and fire. The problem with this model is that just because something is easy to measure does not mean it is worth measuring.

In education, products might look like plays, concerts, readings, DVDs, posters, written papers, tests, drawings, competitions, and the like—anything with a start and finish: "Whew. Glad *that's* over."

Consider "Resume Builders." Students are encouraged to package their experiences (products) in a certain way, and they need to make sure that the number and quality of their packages says something good about them. Many students and parents make the production of packages the focus of high school.

Calling something a product also implies that there is a consumer. In high school, maybe the consumers are teachers, college recruiters, athletic programs, or employers. Products are made to be consumed.

Products in education are not all bad; they are just not the entire learning story. When schools focus only on making a product, they frequently miss the importance of the learning that takes place *during* the process that culminated in the product.

A product without a process is meaningless, evidenced by the number of unimpressive people with impressive resumes. Chances are good that those resumes are laden with products, but lacking in meaningful and learningful processes to back them up.

THE LEARNING JOURNEY (THE PROCESS)

Learning is a journey. Journeys are filled with trials, frustrations, with quests for information and emotional support. *The Lord of the Rings* would be considerably less impressive if Sam and Frodo boarded a plane and flew first class into Mordor. The journey is what made the product (the destruction of the One Ring) meaningful.

Knowing the stages of the learning process—even just knowing that there *are* stages to the learning process—gives learners confidence that whatever they feel at any point is okay, that trials and tribulations are part of the learning journey. The product becomes the symbol of everything that was sacrificed, struggled with, and learned on the journey.

Even so, product and process together do not guarantee powerful learning (changes that move you toward the person you dream of becoming). To accomplish powerful learning, process and the product must align with a meaningful purpose. The struggles during the journey *must* be present, which requires that the purpose be important enough to overcome learning hardships.

COMMUNITY

Humans need Love and Belonging (search Maslow's Hierarchy of Needs online for the others). Building community in the classroom (or on a team) attempts to help participants meet that need in explicit ways. In most classrooms community building is not an intentional part of the curriculum.

Many teams have structures in place to connect individuals to the team: same clothes, same language, and frequently a shared vision for team members. While those structures may exist, the connections to human needs are usually implicit rather than planned.

One strength of teams (and strong communities) is that they implicitly require diversity—different people need to be good at different things. A soccer team cannot have eleven sweepers and be successful. Great teams make explicit the need for diversity, and connect and acknowledge those differences to team and learning success.

Community in Brainball (TE) goes beyond wishful thinking. The teacher (coach) must plan, organize, assess, talk, and model "community" every day. Only then can it be a useful tool for helping meet people's needs. Otherwise, those efforts are perceived as "nice" but not valued, interesting but not learningful.

PURPOSE

The purpose for the product, the process, and the community needs to be explicit and relevant. It needs to be detailed enough to visualize. Purpose needs to be the number one criteria for how the product, the process, and community-building activities are selected.

The purpose of Brainball (TE) (and education as a whole) is to create self-actualized participants in a democratic society. Brainball (TE) is but one thread in a complex tapestry (the others being the additional content areas)—and the key to Brainball (TE) is to teach in a way that makes the teacher/coach dispensable.

Brainball (TE) is a game to be played by people, and people are defined by their beliefs. Explicitly focusing on a student's dispositions (defined as the way that they tend to act under pressure) is what makes the game so personal and effective.

Dispositions are based in beliefs—about self, about others, about how the world functions. Brainball (TE) is meant to take into account and then make visible not only people's dispositions, but also the belief systems by which those dispositions are created and maintained. Peter Senge (1990) states that "structures of which you are unaware hold you prisoner." A person cannot be self-actualized if they are unaware of their deepest beliefs.

As any experienced teacher knows firsthand, one can't force anyone else to learn anything (learning defined as a change in thoughts, beliefs, or actions). Teachers can force students to memorize lines, can threaten students with tests, evaluations, and public humiliation (a poor performance), but learning—that is always a personal choice.

Learning is a hugely personal undertaking. Most people learn to take care of themselves on a basic level out of necessity (a man learns to eat because he is hungry and will die if he does not), but self-actualization is a continual choice. When people deal with complex learning experiences, they have to talk about it, figure out how to do it again, or how to avoid that specific consequence. Learning is also developmental, which means that each person should be taught as an individual who is physiologically changing over time.

So, returning to the goal of education: "to create self-actualized participants in a democratic society" (Kolis, 2011); knowing all of this, how can anyone teach someone else to be self-actualized? It is impossible.

What teachers can do is create experiences (ask questions, focus on specific ideas, ask them to see things from multiple perspectives) that allow for certain types of personal growth to occur. They can teach the process as well as a product (self-actualization is a product like any other) in the support group of a community. They can teach skills that are useful for the continued learning journey, and they can help people examine their journey as well as their destination.

SELF-ACTUALIZATION

Time for another explanation: "Self-actualization" is dynamic. It has as many definitions as there are people. Self-actualization is going to look and feel different for every person. In Maslow's Hierarchy of Needs, self-actualization rests on the top of the pyramid; perhaps that's a good place to start.

Self-actualization is a *need*. It is built into us, standard issue; it is a physiological thing. A need is some thing or state people are biochemically compelled to seek—people are compelled to meet their needs as best as they can, even if they don't know exactly what they are striving for.

There are other needs that must be satisfied first, like safety, food, water, shelter, love, and belonging, but those are not the pinnacle. Why is it that no matter how wealthy a culture is, there are always unhappy people? Why can't people settle down with the basic needs and enjoy it? Self-actualization means the full realization of one's potential.

Trying to define "self-actualization" is pretty murky, so instead of a hard-and-fast definition, here are some characteristics of people who have been identified as self-actualized:

1. *Acceptance and realism*: People who are self-actualized have the ability and confidence in themselves to view life neither optimistically nor pessimistically, and be okay with what they see. They are aware of their own imperfections (and those of others), but since they are on a personal learning journey, they are more focused on moving ahead. They use today's information to change who, what, where, and how they are going to further their learning journey.

They also accept the fact that sometimes what they think is wrong—their current knowledge or skills or dispositions are misguided or incorrect. But that's okay since everything they think they know, can do, or believe are just placeholders for more complex thoughts that may occur later and with more experiences. They use today as the foundation for their next learning cycle.

2. *Problem-centering*: People who are self-actualized are also solution oriented (versus being only analytic or whiners). They are concerned with

solving problems: their own, other peoples' problems, and finding solutions to the problems in the world. If they have been blessed with excellent mentors and guides for their learning journeys, they address problems from a systems point of view rather than merely cause and effect.

They focus on solutions and see each "problem" as a personal responsibility and ethical issue. They do it because they believe "it is the right thing to do."

3. *Spontaneity*: People identified as self-actualized are spontaneous in internal thoughts (connecting ideas that have not been connected before) and outward behaviors, where they demonstrate a willingness to fail. While they can follow the rules, they are not confined by tradition or norms.

They believe that the problems of today are the result of the solutions of yesterday. They are open and unconventional, seeing other's perspectives as enhancing their personal worldview. They believe that rules are boundaries made by man and, therefore, they can be changed when new solutions are called for.

4. *Autonomy and solitude*: While self-actualized people may or may not be socially driven, they do have a high need for independence and privacy. They need time and space to focus on their individual potential and learning. What they really need is "reflective time" or think time. They need time to look at life without their lens of self-protection (ego, power, best light). They need to find out where they are on their learning journey and whether or not a change in plans is called for. They also need time and space to ponder "how else?"

5. *Continued freshness of appreciation*: One of the most interesting aspects of people who are identified as self-actualized is their ability and capacity to view the world around them with a continued sense of appreciation, wonder, and awe. They see simple experiences as the source of inspiration and pleasure. They do not need "more," or "fancier," or "more exclusive" experiences; they see beauty every day and in every place. It is their "way of life."

6. *Peak experiences*: Self-actualized people recognize their moments of intense joy, wonder, awe, and ecstasy. They use those experiences as a means to lead to personal inspiration, acknowledgment of strengths, or as opportunities for renewal or for personal transformation.

They have the ability to "arrive at a place and see it for the first time," no matter how often they have previously visited that place.

A quick note: No one expects K–12 students to become self-actualized. Few people of any age actually achieve self-actualization, and certainly no one whose hormones are changing hour to hour. The point is rather that it is important that *teachers* know what they are striving for (what is the purpose for their students?).

Ultimately Brainball (TE) asks that teachers teach three things at the same time: the product (content), the process (thinking like a thespian), and community (working effectively with others). It is the teacher/coach's job to create the learning opportunities for their students to develop the dispositions, knowledge, and skills so that when they get to the point in their lives when they are ready and able, that they have the habits of mind to grow into their highest potential.

That sounds intimidating. Luckily, small changes can exert enormous leverage. Brainball (TE) is a game. Like every game, Brainball (TE) espouses its own specific set of *dispositions*, *knowledge*, and *skills*. To fully understand the game, one must fully understand each of these sets

Chapter Three

Brainball (TE)

Beliefs (Dispositions)

The term "disposition" is defined by *Merriam-Webster's Dictionary* (2002) as the "tendency to act in certain ways under certain situations." That means dispositions are a person's "go-to" behavior set when things get tense. They are more than knowledge issues (theory, scripts, and content) and more than skills (specific behavior sets). Dispositions are the enactment of a person's deepest beliefs. Dispositions are what make people individuals.

Students' dispositions are the ways in which they address their basic human needs, from having enough food and water, to love and belonging. They are drawn from the students' life experiences, families, genetics, and ambitions. Focusing on dispositions, that is, focusing on what makes students human, is the root of making material relevant. If dispositions are the foundation of a person's actions, then learning experiences need to focus on dispositions rather than merely knowledge and skills. If students do not "revert" (lives outside the classroom) to what has been taught (in the classroom), have they in fact "learned" anything?

In theater classrooms (as well as in most other classrooms), a disposition-focused model is pretty rare, but in athletics it happens fairly regularly. Certain sets of actions and beliefs have been explained, practiced, and reviewed so often that they have become habits of mind (and body).

> *Ben's Story: When I played soccer in college, one of the first things we did at the beginning of each year was sit down and talk about our goals for the year. There were the usual athletics team goals like, "we want to have a winning record," but we also focused on dispositional issues like:*
>
> - *Our Junior Varsity squad will be the best in the conference (meaning we will invest time in our younger players)*

- *If there are problems with eligibility (violations, drinking, low grades) it is the responsibility of the player to approach the coach before anyone else (take responsibility for your actions)*
- *We will work harder than any other team (focus on the things you can control, not the things you can't)*
- *We are a team of hard-playing gentlemen (never let the game make you a worse person)*

Because of these beliefs, our team was more than just a sports-playing apparatus. The team helped us to improve ourselves as well as improve our soccer skills.

People play games for many different reasons. Some play because they think of them as fun, some because they view them as a creative outlet, some for the relationships with others, some for power (to be victorious over others), and some because it fills the time and gives them something to do. In other words, playing games can help meet people's needs.

The game of Brainball (TE) therefore has an explicit "needs" orientation, which is aligned with the core purpose of theater—the expression of the human experience through representative actions. That means that the teacher uses theater as a methodology for learning about yourself (thus enhancing their quality of life).

This matters because outside of school, students wonder about moral dilemmas, about who they are, about what they might be like if they lived somewhere else. Their life focuses on doing the best they can—and deal with life's questions and concerns. They continually seek to express themselves (find their identity) and frequently don't have a structured approach or safe space for effectively doing this. They revert to areas of comfort, sources that they know: friends, television, social media, and the daily bombardment of advertisements (whether they want to encounter them or not).

Each external source leads them to a series of imitations, both in appearance and behavior. Often they combine different looks or behaviors, sometimes unaware they are doing so, trying to find the expression that they feel fits "best." While they find success in various forms in doing this, theater provides a structure and exploration that helps them discover the deeper sources of this need for expression. The process is not short and sweet, but does provide a more structured way for them to discover what it is they are trying to express.

Each type of game develops certain dispositions. Brainball (TE) is important because this particular game provides people with mechanisms for self-reflection and for expressing their experiences in articulate and precise ways. Each person will use this power differently because each person has different experiences and dispositions.

Brainball (TE) is intended to empower the learner. It helps students figure out their strengths and weaknesses. It helps them own their own lives. Being part of a great team also means that students know how to work productively and effectively within a group.

To take on the role of "being theatrical" means to exhibit specific dispositions when working with others and when expressing new thoughts, beliefs, or experiences.

Learning the game of Brainball (TE) means to enhance the quality of a person's life—no matter where they are. It is one way to view life, not just in theater classrooms. And when played well, it allows each individual to identify their own strengths and weaknesses, to discover their passions and to discover what they need to learn next to live toward their passions. They become the owners of their own lives in conscious ways, accepting the consequences of the choices they've made.

Creating learning opportunities that develop into habits of mind (dispositions) requires deep, intentional, and explicit instruction at the belief level; growth needs to spring from the students' personal beliefs. At the deepest level, powerful beliefs about and in themselves (such as those listed below) will set them up for their journey toward self-actualization and the purpose of Brainball (TE):

1. I am creative (and so are other people).
2. I can make good decisions using the appropriate criteria for the decision (critical thinking).
3. Everyone (including me) acts in ways that meet their needs.
4. We know more as a community than as a collection of individuals.
5. Everyone owns their own learning (they are responsible for their own journeys).
6. Reflection is key (helps me align where I am to where I want to be).

1. I am creative (and so are other people).

Being creative is difficult, especially as adults. Adults have learned to separate the world into the realistic and the unrealistic, and why not? It is a survival skill to recognize and understand patterns. If you ask an adult to come up with as many ways as possible to use a paperclip, he might come up with, "Uh, clipping paper, lock pick, and, uh..."

But if one were to ask a kid the same thing, he'd think for a moment and ask, "is it made of rubber? Is it fifty feet tall? Is it a living paperclip?" Kids haven't seen as many patterns as adults, and so there isn't any reason why a paperclip can't be fifty feet tall and alive.

Being creative means being open to other ways of thinking, acting, believing, and considering options, and alternatives with no preconceived notions.

It's hard, as adults, because we think we know so much. We know enough to survive, so what benefit could looking at other options possibly yield?

Creativity is also a diversity issue—it takes creativity to be empathetic. Students need to be able to see an issue from someone else's point of view; they need to understand that others' experiences, the patterns that they have been exposed to, are different than and as valid as their own.

Creativity means to defer judgment (judgment is the opposite of creativity). Nothing stops a brainstorming session faster than someone who can't suspend his/her judgment.

> *Mickey's Story:* I once went to a meeting called by a person of power and was told it was to be a "brainstorming" session. Well, I like being creative, know the rules of how to brainstorm effectively and was interested in actually finding a solution to the task at hand.
>
> *So I participated fully. I added to the ideas of others, I was wild and thought outside the box, I was looking for as many right answers as possible. I was having fun.*
>
> *Five minutes into the session the "leader" told me to be quiet and that we would now add ideas in turn, going around the circle until we were "successful."*
>
> *At that point I realized we were not in fact looking for new solutions, we were looking to discover the answer they had already selected!*

None of this is to say that adults cannot be creative—just that it might take a little more work. Thinking creatively is a skill that can be learned just like any other skill. Creativity is both a gift and a teachable and learnable skill (according to Gary Davis [2004], some examples of creative strategies include: brainstorming, SCAMPER, analogies, visualization, reverse brainstorming, and more).

If a person believes that he is creative, then he will more likely give creative tasks the time, effort, and resources they need in the search for new solutions. He will *act* creatively!

2. I can make good decisions using the appropriate criteria for the decision (critical thinking).

Being able to think critically is the art of making decisions using decision-specific criteria. The criteria by which one makes decisions vary depending on the discipline and the task at hand. How well one knows and uses criteria of a given field when making a decision is a skill that separates the experts from the novices and evaluations from opinions.

Making decisions based upon criteria (rather than luck, what your friends said, or trial and error) allows people to view their lives with more control (and that means power). Every day people make hundreds if not thousands of decisions—about what to wear, buy, eat, and say/hear/ignore. Knowing the criteria for a nice outfit and making decisions based on that understanding is what separates the sharp dressers from the unaccessorized masses.

Believing that different criteria work best for different kinds of decisions pushes the individual from impulse to consideration. The search moves from deciding quickly with little information to finding the appropriate criteria for the decision and then applying them in rational ways.

The more complex the decision, the more important it is to find and use the very best criteria (expert level). Using excellent criteria increases the probability of making decisions that work for you.

3. Everyone (including me) acts in ways that meet their needs.

Humans act in ways that meet their needs. So the question is: "Which need is this behavior meeting?" and then, "Might there be a better, more effective way to meet that need?"

Telling someone to change some behavior that is meeting his needs perfectly is totally unproductive. Punishment is supposed to solve this by changing the person's immediate need to "avoiding punishment." However, chances are good that the punishable action is meeting a much deeper need than "avoiding punishment."

How people decide to meet their needs (their behaviors) might not be the most effective way to go about meeting those needs, just the most obvious. To a child, crying might seem the best way to meet a need; but as the child grows and learns, she'll find that asking politely for a glass of juice accomplishes her goal more effectively.

But changing one's behavior is not always obvious and easy. Sometimes people need help replacing a flawed strategy (that for the short term meets their needs) with a more productive strategy.

Being aware that one's behaviors are the best attempt to meet one's needs is the beginning of awareness. It moves the individual from chaos to choices, and with choices come power and responsibility.

4. We know more as a community than as a collection of individuals.

Community is a way of interacting with others that meets multiple needs and works toward a "shared goal or vision." When a classroom functions as a community, the students understand that there is a "good of the group," and that the learning of the group as a whole will benefit them as an individual (think Win–Win).

The opposite of community is a competitive classroom, where students view the group as an impediment to their individual success. A consumer theater classroom is filled with students singing or playing exactly the way the teacher wants them to, with the teacher at the top on the podium, the sole source, and provider of knowledge. A community focus shifts the role of the student from "consumer" to "contributor."

A classroom community values the differences that lie within the group and view them as a strength. A community requires or invites every individual to contribute to the whole, and by doing so, find his place in the group. Being part of a community means having a place. Every person in a community knows who he/she is and in what way he/she makes the group stronger.

Competition is based on scarcity. Students compete over solos, recognition, grades, and attention. There is only so much "stuff" to go around, so students have to fight for it. The stronger students rise to the surface (their strengths match the class requirements for success) and the weaker fade into the background (their strengths are at odds with the classroom structure).

The basis of community (at the belief level) is "enough-ness." There is enough success, joy, love, and recognition for everyone. Everyone has a gift and everyone has a place in the community. The teacher's task is to be creative enough to help each student find his place.

> *Ben's Story: This last summer I was directing a dance show composed of high schoolers and a couple of adults for good measure. We'd spent the summer making the show together from the ground up and it was our final performance. But one of the performers (one of the adults no less) didn't show up—he wouldn't answer his phone and we couldn't track him down. We were freaking out.*
>
> *As 170 people filled the theatre and 5 minutes until we were supposed to start, the students re-choreographed the entire show. They re-structured scenes, they taught and took each other's parts, they figured out where and how props were going to go for which scenes. We went onstage with a brand new show and different parts. They behaved more professionally than the professionals I'd hired. And no one in the audience ever knew.*
>
> *Because we'd spent the entire summer experimenting with and supporting one another, because we listened to each other's ideas and empathized in a safe space, we overcame a really stressful situation with flying colors.*

Community matters because it meets human needs (love and belonging). The more people compete with one another, the less opportunity there will be to discover strengths, passions, and ways to contribute to the greater good.

5. Everyone owns their own learning (they are responsible for their own journeys).

Learning is defined as a change in thoughts, beliefs, or actions. To switch things around a little, learning hasn't taken place unless the learner behaves, thinks, or views life differently.

This also means that one is allowed to choose what one learns. And since learning is a choice—it is also a responsibility, but stick with choice for now—each person owns the consequences of his/her learning. People have not truly learned unless they own the consequences of their decisions (no excuses).

It is the teacher's responsibility to structure an environment wherein students can learn from their situations by owning the consequences. Furthermore, it is the teacher's responsibility to make sure that those consequences are developmentally appropriate. Failing and learning from one's failures is the only way to build self-confidence and trust in oneself.

This belief (learning is each individual's choice) changes how teachers should go about the job of "teaching." They should begin with what the students think they already know and then create learning opportunities that cause them to rethink, reconsider, and reevaluate. And teachers need to do all that in a supportive classroom environment.

6. Reflection is key (helps me align where I am to where I want to be).

Self-aware people can look at themselves. They can examine their own thoughts, words, and actions, from a place outside of themselves. Objectivity is impossible, but that knowledge, plus making the acknowledgment of new perspectives a habit rather than a chore, is a direct route to meaningful learning.

Reflection positions learning as centrally important. The opposite of reflection is stagnation, or inaction. Reflection inspires action. Reflection is the power to see (a) this is where I am right now, (b) that is where I want to be, and (c) this is how I intend to get there from here.

While reflection seems like the least important of all the learning processes, it is actually the most important. It is the power to plan the next step. It is what all the processes taught in school have in common, no matter the discipline—reflect. And yet, it never seems to be the focus.

Reflection is the step wherein learning actually takes place. Runners don't know how to improve their technique as they are running—they become better by watching a film of themselves, or listening to their coach and saying to themselves, "This is how I do better"; if learning is the "what" of making changes in oneself, reflection is the "how."

Reflecting upon learning experiences (without guilt) requires: (a) the ability to see different perspectives (being curious), (b) looking for criteria that determine effective choices, (c) comparing the new perspectives to the old ones, (d) feeling supported enough by others to see what they see, and (e) seeing that experience as neither good nor bad but as part of one's learning journey. Each discipline uses discipline-specific language to describe its ideal set of dispositions, though in spirit they remain the same. Science might word (f) reflection is key differently—maybe "Record, reflect, retest" (or something). In chapter 6, we list and elaborate on the theatrical versions of these general dispositions. They are:

1. I am creative and so are you (how else?)
2. Audience mindset
3. Everyone acts in ways that meet their needs
4. Yes > No
5. Everyone owns his/her own learning
6. Reflection and revision
7. Be committed to the team-learning journey

ALIGNMENT WITH PURPOSE

Having a clear purpose helps align the process, the product, and the community toward an explicit end in mind. Each piece is important unto itself—and even more important when seen as a collective whole. The purpose of schooling is not to create thespians, college graduates, mechanics, politicians, or any of a thousand other choices. It is to prepare people to live to their own highest potential in ways that meet their needs. It is about preparing people to see where they are, and then to move forward, all the while enjoying the learning journey.

If a person's dispositions are the enactment of their beliefs, then what a person believes matters. People believe what they do because of their experiences, how they process those experiences, and what they chose to learn from them. People at the same place and time may walk away with very different life experiences.

Beliefs are so deeply embedded that very frequently people are unaware that they exist. In fact, it might be easier for a third party to see a person's belief system than the person himself/herself can.

It is possible for anyone to change their dispositions, but only by addressing their beliefs. Knowledge and skills always align to the belief system in place. People learn facts and theories that support their beliefs and learn the skills to enact them.

Choosing to play Brainball (TE) is to focus directly on one way to view the world (one specific belief system). The game *must* to be played over and over again so that people have the time and experiences to learn what the game has to offer to them as individuals.

The game offers the opportunity to learn to "think like this, act like that, and know these things" at the deepest personal levels (self-knowledge). When the game incorporates both creativity and critical thinking, it opens the world for ways to see one's life as a creative exercise and to own one's own life (and that means choices and their consequences—no excuses). It allows for explicit growth toward self-actualization.

Chapter Four

Brainball (TE)
Key Concepts (Knowledge)

Chapter 2 dealt with aligning product, process, and community, which requires a depth of knowledge, some specific skills, and the desire to connect all classroom learning into a relevant, integrated whole. The definition of "knowledge," according to *Merriam-Webster*, is, "applies to the facts or ideas acquired by study, investigation, observation, or experience" which is heavily biased toward some sort of personal interaction with the information.

Knowledge attempts to explain the "WHY" things work the way they do, how the facts are connected into a whole (a concept)—the theory of the thing. It includes the rules, the strategies, the boundaries of the game being played, and all the little factoids that "experts" know. Playing the game makes knowledge worthwhile (if you want to get better at the game) while knowledge makes the game easier to play.

While true in a basic sense, *Merriam-Webster*'s definition could stand some refining for the purposes of this book. Brainball (TE) is a dispositions-focused game—it teaches people so that they may ultimately live to their life's potential. A working definition of knowledge that does not make explicit the humanness of knowledge is flawed.

People own and construct their own knowledge. It exists within a human vessel. In order to "own" knowledge (the WHY things work the way they do), people take facts and put them through a complex humanness; knowledge is colored by prior experiences, belief systems, and everything that makes people who they are. Knowledge is all about the personal connections between the individual and the information at hand.

Knowledge goes beyond the facts. People naturally take facts and connect them to their personal experience; they try and recognize patterns, see connections, and make assumptions about how all the pieces fit together.

They also reflect on what they think they already know, further changing it. Knowledge is not uniform.

A more nuanced way of understanding "knowledge" is to consider the ways in which a person understands something. People use the word "understand" frequently; again the term could use some specificity. The "Dimensions of Understanding" (Kolis, 2012) might provide a more explicit view. There are, in fact, multiple ways to understand something:

1. Concept understanding. This includes all the information, the facts, and how those facts are connected to bigger ideas (concepts).
2. Context understanding. This puts the knowledge into a time and place situation (at that time and at that place, knowing what they knew). Context understanding means to understand from a different perspective (without 20/20 hindsight).
3. Analysis understanding. The ability to break the whole into pieces, and being able to name and identify those pieces is at the heart of analysis.
4. Creativity understanding. Being able to "play" and see things from new perspectives and put the pieces together in novel ways. It means using your current knowledge to create something new.
5. Critical thinking understanding. To be able to make decisions based upon field-appropriate criteria. To know what is most important or most useful at that specific time requires the ability to prioritize according to how an expert would view the situation. Ultimately it means to make decisions like an expert.
6. Application understanding. To put knowledge into action is what differentiates application from theory: the ability to *do* something with one's knowledge.
7. Self-knowledge understanding. The ability to use life experiences to work toward self-actualization. This means to take one's experiences and make them learningful.

Ben's Story: A big part of being a performer is being coached—you stand up and perform while someone watches you. They give advice and notes, and you give it another go, doing your best to make sense of what they said. But performing is really specific to your own body—no one else knows how your voice works, or how it feels when you move. My coach's advice—while I'm sure he was right—was never something I could incorporate fully. I didn't know enough in enough ways about my body to make good sense of his advice.

To overcome this, I started to record myself when I performed. When I did, I saw myself as my coach did—watching, I was able to focus less on how it felt (which is what I'd been doing before), and more on how it appeared (which is what my coach had been trying to get me to know). We'd been understanding the same experience (my performance) in totally different dimensions.

To say that the Dimensions of Understanding is the best and only way to think about knowledge is as misleading as thinking the initial definition of knowledge is sufficient. If knowledge is unique to each human, than offering any definitive classification system at all is dishonest.

Instead, the Dimensions of Understanding is one way of many to consider knowledge and one that provides a useful vocabulary in the context of this book.

THE KEY KNOWLEDGE CATEGORIES

Key knowledge categories are the most basic structures around which *all* information in the game revolves. They provide the essential framework by which students can organize all the information they might learn. All the facts, information, scripts, symbols, the dos and don'ts, fall into these basic categories. In Brainball (TE), the three key knowledge categories are (a) Content Learning, (b) Process Learning, and (c) Community Learning.

1. Content Learning

Content learning includes the facts, the information, the scripts, the symbols, the historical basis, and the connections between the pieces. Most tests and quizzes focus on this type of learning and the terms (the vocabulary) form the basis for how each content area talks and communicates. Content is important as the foundation for thinking—it is just not the only learning that matters.

Each content area that is subdivided has different disciplines and the further your study takes you, the more subdisciplines there are, but all disciplines start with the central concepts, or the elements that are present in every discipline. In theater (the art of representative actions), the central concepts are:

1. The performer in space
2. History and context
3. Representation

They are deliberately broad to encompass all the different parts of theater and performance. Many theater programs teach classes like "Script Analysis," or "Directing," or "Acting," which are all composed of different elements of these three central concepts.

Content learning also meets specific curriculum outcomes set by school districts, states, and national groups. Content learning is all the stuff we ask our students to "know."

All content areas (theater, science, math, language arts, etc.) are held together by three to eight central concepts. Central concepts are those ideas that are found in every discipline (although sometimes the words used to describe that idea are different). Those central concepts are what distinguishes one content area from the next. Making the central concepts clear and explicit to students gives them a clear framework for connecting all the little facts to full and complex concepts.

FACTS AND CENTRAL CONCEPTS

Sometime it's hard to see the forest for the trees, and sometimes hard to see the trees for the forest. Details (individual facts) are important for how they help students understand the central concepts. Those central concepts (the forest) are supported by a million small factoids, the details. Too frequently, teachers get lost in memorizing the minutia of a subject without connecting facts to the concept being taught, the context from which those ideas emerged or learning how to break the forest into little pieces (the trees).

And it works in reverse as well. Building facts into central concepts is useful, as is taking the central concept and breaking it down. When students know the central concept, patterns and predictions become obvious, opening the door for creativity and individuality.

Really, it's a two-way street—without details (the facts), the big pictures are washed out and grainy. Details not only support the central concepts but also are responsible for making those central concepts vibrant and interesting.

For example in soccer, the central concepts are dribbling, passing (includes shooting and receiving), and spatial relationships.

If a coach starts by teaching complex attack strategies, he posits that as the most basic and essential information worth knowing. From there, he has to teach complex defensive strategies—from scratch (without connecting it to things the players already know), since this too is positioned as basic information. Both strategies (attack and defense) are more complex variations of a central concept: spatial relationships.

If the coach had positioned spatial relationships as the basic information, rather than his complex attack and defensive derivatives, he would have established that the two are rooted in the same vocabulary. By teaching his players two (seemingly) unconnected strategies, he has discouraged them from making connections about how they connect and interact with one another. He has made his team less efficient.

Instead of learning a part, and then memorizing when Shakespeare was born, and then blocking a scene (sometime in the same class and with little explanation), central concepts give students the structure and vocabulary to organize and connect the information in their minds.

There are numerous disciplines and subdisciplines of theater and performance (lighting, sound, history, modern, etc.), and each discipline owns its own vocabulary regarding those central concepts. A lighting designer thinks about side lighting, a choreographer thinks about balancing the space—both of which are discipline-specific ways of considering the performer in space.

Naming the central concepts in class (labeling them) allows all learners to make connections between the disciplines and build upon prior student knowledge rather than allowing them to think that what they learned previously has no connection to what they are learning today.

Because if you're a dancer, what's the point in learning script analysis? Without talking about how each is heavily attached to the central concept: Representation (the dancer with his choreography and the scriptwriter with his words), they appear unconnected. When we talk about the central concepts, we free our students to see the connections between disciplines.

The relationship between the big picture and the small pictures should be dynamic. In Brainball (TE), the puzzle is never finished. Puzzles are static, whereas Brainball (TE) builds upon itself. The game is dynamic when there's meaning between the big and small pictures. It is dynamic when it's more than the sum of its parts.

Mickey's Story: In soccer a common play is called "an overlapping run." That means a person who is playing a position different than yours runs into your space and begins to play your position.

This play causes defenders many problems because they have to decide which player they are going to defend.

The reverse is also true. When the ball changes sides, the person who is "overlapped" now has to play a different position.

The game is ever changing!

WHERE TO START?

Organizing for content learning is very much a question of the chicken or the egg. Should the teacher start with the central concept and work toward the facts or begin with facts and build toward the central concepts? When and how will students understand that everything is connected?

For students to learn the interplay between facts and concepts, the teacher has to model the connections that can be made and make those connections explicit to the learners every day (they have to model and label what they expect). That means they themselves have to deeply understand each of the central concepts of theater.

1. Content Learning

Content learning is what most theater classrooms currently focus on teaching—and those facts, scripts, concepts, and ideas are important. They're the basis upon which some really important thinking rests, but they are not (in and of themselves) thinking.

2. Process Learning

Process learning attempts to make explicit the steps that a person takes in going from a human experience to a theatrical story through representative actions. Process learning focuses on "how the game is played," and Brainball (TE) is the game of expression of the human experience through representative actions in a community of learners.

A game is made up of and defined by its rules. Athletes are connected to one another because they use the same set of rules. So too are theater-makers connected to one another by the process of creating and performing their theatrical stories (remember, human stories through representative actions).

Theatrical processes are how an individual navigates and plays with the rules of Brainball (TE). There is a pattern that thespians have to learn if they want to be a functional member of the community. And just like an athlete, the better the thespian understands the rules of the game, the more creative he can be with them.

The rules (the structure the game takes) includes the cans and the can'ts, the dos and the don'ts. Without a set of rules (process), no one would be playing the same game.

It is tempting to think, "Theater" means "scripts." Rather, scripts are the results of people who have "done" theater, and recorded one product of their process. Theater is a process, and the second key knowledge concept (process learning) provides a structure for doing something with the experiences that need to be expressed (content learning).

Process learning also provides a structure for learning outside the theater classroom. It provides a methodology for sharing and expressing the human experience of one's life outside the classroom—and that is powerful learning.

3. Community Learning

Process learning is closely tied to the third key knowledge concept, the role of the theatrical community. If theater is about expressing the human experience through representative actions, the questions "With whom are those experiences uncovered/discovered/analyzed?" and "With whom are those stories shared?" should be addressed.

The theater community includes all the other players of the game and also includes how the players interact: specifically here, the support they provide and the roles they fill. Since the purpose of theater is learning (the expression of the human experience through representative actions), the other players in the theater community function as both teammates and competitors.

Teammates serve as learning colleagues when support is needed intellectually, socially, emotionally, physically, or morally. Everyone must work together and contribute to the shared vision of the group (expressing powerful experiences through representative actions). Everyone needs to contribute something to the whole is a community is to be built.

(Constructive) Competition plays a role by helping players figure what they need to learn next, helps to sharpen their skills, and pushes them to become better. Ultimately from the learning perspective and Brainball (TE), people compete against themselves (against their learning expectations), with the other players functioning as a measuring stick and holding everyone accountable for their own learning.

There are a couple of ways to think about the theater community: First, the theater community as a global whole. Second, the community as it functions on a classroom level.

The global theater community is a natural group. A thespian becomes part of the global community by knowing the rules of the game and contributing. It is not people focused—it is learning focused (the greater goal supersedes individual needs). Diversity is implicitly understood to be a strength based on what learning the individual contributes to the group.

Just as soccer is a world game, so is the community of thespians. People understand the game, its rules, and how the game is to be played nearly everywhere on earth. They play the game with their own cultural bent or emphasis. Some focus on defense, some on creativity, and some on teamwork. Performance varies wildly country to country and culture to culture. It serves different purposes, values different disciplines over others, but no matter what is emphasized, the game remains at its core the same.

On a classroom level, the theater community is a quasi-natural group. Some students are part of the group because they want to or because they believe they have something to contribute, while others participate because their parents or counselors told them to (or because they think it'll be an easy A).

In theater classrooms, the ultimate goal (learning) is often forsaken in favor of performing well for a play or competition. The goal of the game is confused with the way the game is measured. Classrooms are full of humans with flaws and baggage, with the immediate rather than the important driving classroom decisions. In a classroom, it is easy to lose focus on learning (becoming better at the game) and focus instead on the next performance (winning the game).

In traditional theater classrooms, teachers do the teaching/directing and students do the "acting." There is a clear power hierarchy, with the students at the bottom and the teacher at the top. The teacher, as well as the script the teacher distributes, is the most important thing in the room, with meaningful learning happening only occasionally and only by accident.

Poor and average athletic teams are organized the same way: The coach is at the top of the power pyramid, with the athletes doing their best to follow his instructions. The success of the team is gauged only by whether or not they win their games. The team's best players are prominently displayed, with the less skilled further in the background.

Great teams on the other hand utilize their diversity to learn (accomplish) something important—to play the game with joy and meet the needs of each individual, all while striving toward a common goal.

The third key knowledge concept (community learning) is rarely made explicit in theater classrooms. Teachers may think they are training their students to take part in the theater community, but without making it explicit, it feels an awful lot like mindlessly following directions.

Changing a theater classroom from merely performance-focused into a community of learners striving toward a common goal requires a shift in thinking, for both students and teacher. It takes work, but focusing on building community provides students with experiences that shape how they interact, work, and communicate with each other.

Experts understand the game (all dimensions worth) across all three key knowledge concepts (content, process, and community). They understand each key concept and how they interact with others to create and play the game. An expert Brainball (TE) player/coach understands that the game

1. is iterative, which means that the same ideas appear over and over again in varying levels of complexity
2. is dynamic, which means that an expert of the game is able to take the basics of the game, see their complex implications, and modify on the fly
3. appears as steps but isn't; the experience is just too complex for linear description
4. views diversity as a strength: everyone has a job, and everyone has value
5. is meant to be fun (appropriately challenging)—and that means to meet player's needs in developmentally appropriate ways.

Knowledge is personal; it must be earned. It isn't just what a person knows but also how he learned it, who was there when he learned what he learned, and on and on. Great teachers (and coaches) design and construct explicit learning around the three key knowledge concepts of content learning, process learning, and community learning.

Chapter Five

Brainball (TE)
Skills

Skills and knowledge are different. Knowledge is big, and soft, and abstract. Knowledge is information translated through each human person because each human has his or her own way of understanding each thing. There is nothing big, soft, or abstract about skills. Skills are specific and objective. Skills are tools. A tool's value is in how efficiently and effectively it does the job for which it was designed.

Knowledge and skills are, however, linked. According to *Merriam-Webster*, a "skill" is defined as "the ability to use one's knowledge effectively and readily in execution or performance." Skills are the application of knowledge—the ability to *do* things with what you know.

Skills are what happen when you do something with theory. Skills in any discipline are derived from a specific need—the need to express something, solve something, think in certain ways, prove something, create something, fix something, or design something.

Students already know the importance of developing skills—it's so basic that defining it actually takes some work. Those skills that people develop are engendered and given meaning by the rules of the game (whatever game they are playing). For example, the only reason that soccer players learn to dribble the ball (skill) is because they aren't allowed to use their hands (rules). Rules give the skills meaning. Actors learn to project (skills) because they are performing for an audience who needs to hear them (rules).

Practice is the action of repeating and (hopefully) refining the performance of a specific skill. It is the connecting point between two otherwise useless things. Skills are how a mechanic goes from knowing what's wrong with a car (knowledge) to fixing the car. It is the difference between knowing what a thespian does and being (or acting like) a thespian. After a coach talks strategy for half an hour and all the athletes head out onto the field to enact the strategies—what do they call that? Practice.

"Skills" are not just motor skills. Learning to think in a certain way is a skill. The ability to synthesize, summarize, make generalizations from diverse experiences, use criteria to rank items, identify the pieces of a whole, interpret sounds, think reflectively, and compose in ways that communicate one's experiences are all skills. Each way of thinking is a specific skill or skill set.

It's not enough to simply have a skill. Skill issues are connected on a basic level to knowledge and disposition issues. One must have a skill, but it also helps to know when, where, how, why (theory) it works the way it does and then choose to use it (disposition). Skills, knowledge, and dispositions are interrelated and iterative.

SKILLS AND PRACTICE IN THE GAME

Practice is supposed to create habits of mind and body for practitioners to fall back on during the game. A sport isn't fun until players can stop worrying about whether they can make that kick and start worrying about how the specific kick will give them an advantage. It's like the saying that goes: "If all you have is a hammer, everything looks like a nail." You use the skills you have to solve the problems you have—but the more skills you have, the more efficiently you can solve problems. An expert focuses not on whether his tool will work but which tool will do the job the most efficiently and effectively.

Skills are habits, and habits are built by repetition; it takes time, effort, and concentration to make a skill a "habit of mind or of muscle memory." Consider flossing: a good habit. The knowledge is that flossing is good for you. The skill is getting the stuff out from between one's teeth. The disposition is that you believe that health and happiness are connected. The habit is getting oneself out of bed every morning and heading to the bathroom to floss. That's hard. That takes practice.

The phrase "practice makes perfect" is untrue upon close examination. Perfection does not spring from imperfection. Practicing something incorrectly again and again doesn't lead to perfection. The effort and concentration that a person puts into practice will ultimately determine their future skill mastery and performance during a competition. Only perfect practice makes perfect.

A more apt phrasing might be "practice makes permanent." The entire point of practice is to know something well enough that one could perform the skill without thinking (a habit of mind or body), leaving the mind free to focus on more important and complex issues. Saying that practice makes permanent implies that practice is a base upon which other skills are built and to which other skills are connected, whereas saying practice makes perfect implies that skills are developed in a void, unconnected to theory or the rest of the game.

"PLAY (BRAIN)BALL!"

To *do* inquiry—that is, to *play* Brainball (TE) like any other sport, the player needs to know and be able to do each of the individual skills. Inquiry relies on many skills, with each step of expressing the human experience through representative actions requiring a different one. For both athletes and thespians, the more sophisticated the game, the more refined the required tool.

At seven years of age, the ability to dribble the ball down the field will make a star. At twenty-two years of age, in a faster, more complex game, that same skill will still warrant stardom—as long as the sophistication with which the player dribbles that ball down that field has grown with the sophistication of the game they're playing now. Dribbling is a tool that gets more and more specific and complex as the game becomes more specific and complex.

But theater is a game different from soccer and requires different skills. Some theater tools are:

Observing	Being curious	Creating problem statements
Arranging	Recognizing interactions, asking "why"	
Phrasing	Composing	Spatial awareness
Being creative	Listening	Responding to the director
Experimenting	Interpreting style	
Reacting/responding to a turn of a phrase	Saying the words	
Scansion	Projection	Diction
Flexibility		

Using appropriate criteria for the task at hand (genres, eras, etc.)
Recognizing parameters (lighting, set, cues, etc.)
Communicating effectively; nonverbal communication (breath, eye contact, lifting)
Connecting text into phrases
Recognizing variations, patterns, sequences

It's a long list, but without a multiplicity of skills, it's impossible to *do* theater. Players who excel (and have the most fun) are the players who have the largest toolbox, in both athletics and theater.

TEAM SKILLS

Every game requires knowledge about content, process, and community (the key knowledge concepts), and there are skills that go along with each of them. Most of the skills thus far (see above list) deal with the first two key knowledge concepts, content learning, and process learning, But the skills that make up community learning are no less important and are less frequently addressed in the classroom. The ability to be an effective team member requires the following interpersonal skills or skill sets:

1. Verbal skills (speaking, listening, reading, and exhibiting appropriate body language)
2. Use of appropriate criteria to make expert-level decisions for the situation
3. The ability to differentiate between knowledge, skill, and disposition issues
4. Align personal (individual) goals/choices with team goals/choices
5. A success orientation
6. Find ways to put the right people in the right place
7. Build trust between and with all the individuals on the team

Sometimes great teams just occur—they exist through "luck." Brainball (TE) is designed to create great teams with consistency, which requires the knowledge, skills, and dispositions of working together to accomplish something important.

Learning (especially about oneself) is usually seen as relevant. Brainball (TE) players who learn the knowledge, practice the skills, and then choose to act differently are on their journey toward meeting their ever-changing needs (self-actualization) in a rapidly changing world.

Section Two

PREPARING TO COACH THE GAME

Great coaches are also great learners. They are "students of the game" no matter how long they coach. They continue learning about the knowledge of the game, developing the skills of their players, and focusing on helping their players grow into positive, compassionate human beings. They see the game as a tool for learning rather than the whole point of the activity.

And since the game is the tool for learning it also makes sense that learning be both intentional and explicit. Intentional means learning is planned, organized, and assessed with the end in mind (no wishful thinking). Explicit means that content, process, and community are named and that students come to own that language and power for themselves.

Great coaches also see the game as "intellectual fun." They focus on helping the players learn rather than just perform and they try to make themselves dispensable. Ultimately, great coaches coach people—and (rather surprisingly) their teams seem to be very successful.

Coaching any game at the highest level of performance requires a clear sense of purpose (what matters most), using the game as a way to teach things that are important, and seeing differences as a strength of the team rather than a problem to be fixed. In the best case, coaches also foster a climate of teamness, where everyone contributes (and everyone is appreciated) in their own personal way. Great coaches are a lot like great teachers. They make a difference.

Becoming a great coach of Brainball (TE) requires a disposition-first outlook (chapter 6), and a willingness to have the players (students) play the game to see where they are and what they need to learn next (chapter 7). Chapter 8 points to the need for competitions to inform everyone how much they have learned and how deep that learning has been. Chapter 9 emphasizes that there is in fact a time, a place, and a sequence that allows learning to grow as quickly and deeply as possible and chapter 10 talks about the importance of explicit communication.

Chapter Six

Tip 1
Keep the End in Mind

In Stephen Covey's book, *The 7 Habits of Highly Effective People*, Habit 2 is listed as "Begin with the End in Mind." It means to keep one's eyes on the prize, avoid distraction when other ideas emerge, and live intentionally. It is easier said than done.

Many people "kind of know" what they want, but few have written it down, shared it, or used it to drive their daily decisions. Keeping the end-in-mind means that it is the criterion by which every decision is made—a decision either advances an end-in-mind or it doesn't.

The end-in-mind for Brainball (TE) is for students to grow highly effective at

1. the study of the human experience, especially their own (this includes teamwork), and
2. expressing that human experience through representative actions.

These two ideas include content learning, process learning, and community learning.

Keeping the end-in-mind means that every instructional decision the teacher makes (really every single one) either moves students toward that goal or it doesn't.

In *The Fifth Discipline*, Peter Senge uses the idea of "leverage" to simplify big changes. Leverage (give me a long-enough lever and I can move the world) allows teachers to do lots of work with manageable amounts of effort. In Brainball (TE) this means that teachers should focus their energies where they will create the greatest amount of (future) learning—and that means working on dispositions (one's behavior under pressure).

Dilemma: You cannot teach dispositions. You can, however, put students in situations where a certain disposition will best meet their needs. That is what effective coaching is: designing and implementing experiences wherein people can choose to change themselves (change means learning) (remember—explicitly and intentionally).

From an educational point of view, this is pretty radical. Theater classes in general teach skills first and always, knowledge second and sometimes, and dispositions hardly ever. Teachers don't often expect students to use classes to benefit their real lives outside the classroom on a daily basis (or at least not explicitly).

This however is a real bummer because teaching appropriate dispositions allows students to connect the knowledge and skills taught in any subject (not just theater) to their immediate lives (how they will go about meeting their needs). And suddenly, making the choice to learn is easy.

The dispositions that Brainball (TE) credits are life skills, not just game skills. Owning one's learning, understanding your human experience, being able to express the human experience, and learning how to work within a community are strengths that everyone uses every day.

It is not the coach's job to make sure his players make his preferred choice every single time. Rather, it is the coach's job to construct scenarios from which her players see the advantages of behaving a certain way. By the time the big game comes around, confident coaches never need to give their players answers from the sidelines. By then, the players have learned how to make their own decisions (they are the ones playing the game)—and learn from the consequences.

You (the educator) will not be there when your students make their most important life decisions. You will not be there when their parents are fighting, when they are learning to drive, or when they decide that they are in love for the first time. You cannot save them from the natural consequences of their choices. You cannot shout answers at them from the sidelines. You can, however, prepare them to examine their human experiences, how to express these experiences through representative actions, and how to work effectively with others. These are life skills that are always relevant.

Teaching dispositions first allows students to play the game the way it was intended to be played. This includes developing the moral, ethical, and community-focused aspects of the game. A referee enforces the rules of the game—but the best teams never need a ref because they know implicitly what the point of the game is—to improve.

THE NEXT STEP

Frequently the object of a team sport is to "win," but that misses the point of the game entirely. If "winning" is what it is all about, then only the state/

national champions have successful seasons. Teaching dispositions help focus the learning on individual and team growth. And although "winning" is not the explicit goal of a learning-focused team, learning to play the game increases the chances of victory.

Once the teacher has positioned dispositions as the focal point, the ultimate end-in-mind, the teacher must start showing how those dispositions connect to discipline-specific knowledge and skills. Since Brainball (TE) is a game, and games are iterative and dynamic, the players get to start slow. Learning is not a one-time occurrence; a class will address the same issues over and over again, each time with more depth and complexity.

Each human creates knowledge for himself or herself, and therefore, good coaches create experiences for them to process and reflect upon. Students should be able to ask their own questions, and discover their own answers in theatrically appropriate ways, using discipline-specific dispositions.

THE DISPOSITIONS

Chapter 3 was a general discussion about disposition-focused learning, the end-in-mind being the student's "Self-Actualization." They were:

1. I am creative (and so are other people).
2. I can make good decisions using the appropriate criteria for the decision (critical thinking).
3. Everyone (including me) acts in ways that meet their needs.
4. We know more as a community than as a collection of individuals.
5. Everyone owns their own learning (they are responsible for their own journeys).
6. Reflection is key (helps me align where I am to where I want to be).
7. Be committed to the team-learning journey.

These are great for a general discussion, but each discipline values and phrases these dispositions in a slightly different way. For theater:

1. I am creative and so are you (how else?)
2. Audience mindset
3. Everyone acts in ways that meet their needs
4. Yes > No
5. Everyone owns their own learning
6. Reflection and revision
7. Be committed to the team-learning journey

1. I Am Creative and So Are You (How Else?)

A belief in creativity allows you to ask, "How else?" What a question. Asking "how else?" is the root of theater. Theater, which is not the human experience, but rather the human experience (re)imagined. How else? What would my life be like if X? How would I react? What would it be like to move like that? How does that feel?

Creativity is an exercise in empathy. You have to believe that there is value in other people's experiences; you have to believe that you can learn from and believe in—if not *fully* understand at least *try to* understand people who are not you. Without that belief, theater is just the staging of an autobiography.

When a group of people ask, "how else?" politics goes out the window. People play to their strengths, speak frankly about what they think and believe, and try to reach shared understanding when they believe that they share an essential humanness with the rest of the group.

This disposition embeds the discipline with the idea that theater is not only *about* the human experience but is also a *result of* the human experience.

TEAM EXAMPLES: I AM CREATIVE AND SO ARE YOU (HOW ELSE?)

Poor/average teams: Players rarely see themselves or others in their work. They do not ask questions. Coaches rely heavily on "traditional wisdom." The coach decides what work to do, what is good, and what is bad with little explanation. Quality of work is based on how well skills are used and little else. The coach does not consider whether the audience will care about the show or not.

Good teams: Players try to make work that is "good," and that people will "like," but it is unclear exactly what this means. The coach makes occasional comparisons of real life to the work. How the team feels about the work is determined by what the audience thinks about it.

Great teams: Players see themselves in the work and in their peers and make efforts to understand and be understood. Students know when to listen and when to speak up. The coach allows team members to make decisions within a larger framework. Things are not wrong or right—instead the coach adds new information and allows the team to revise and restructure.

2. Audience Mindset

Theater is defined by the audience. There is no performance, no theater, without an (implied) viewer of some kind or another.

Because theater uses representations of the human experience, representations that we hope communicate to people that don't have that experience firsthand, theater's power is limited not by what human experience the theater is based on but rather how effectively the performers are able to communicate that experience to another party.

Theatre needs a watcher and needs to be watched. The audience is primary. The theater-maker is a translator, taking her own human experiences, applying the skills of her discipline to them, and presenting them to an audience who will *feel something.*

> *Ben's Story: Being critiqued is part of performing. You tend to take what you can out of them; some are useful and you can use to improve, some are not. But the harshest critique I've ever received is when an audience member says, "I can't believe you memorized all of those lines!"*
>
> *It isn't meant to be cruel—it's mostly meant as a compliment. Though the performance did make that audience member feel something, even if it was just about text memorization, I can't help but feel that I didn't do my job. My job is to make you laugh, or cry, to get angry or to change somehow. If all I did was impress you with how I use a basic tool of the trade (memorization), I'd better figure out how I can improve.*

None of which means that the audience has to be *happy*. Audience mindset isn't about judging a piece's value or content. Lots of theater is entertaining, yes, but just as valuable is theater that is upsetting, angering, sickening, or whatever else you decide. But theater is a relationship between watcher and viewer, and the viewer expects you to be intentional.

TEAM EXAMPLES: AUDIENCE MINDSET

Poor/average teams: Players use game as personal therapy. Players use other teammates to validate their own personal experiences. Players interpret critiques on work as personal criticism. There is a feeling of "if I feel it, it must be right." Coaches do not reference theatrical tools. Coaches conflate theatrical skill and "being emotional."

Good teams: Players understand that there's a difference between "feeling" something and "effectively showing" showing something but do not always recognize it when it happens. Coaches struggle to get their students to "leave their problems at the door."

Excellent teams: Players use their own experiences, and the experiences of their teammates to inform and explore their work. There is a feeling of "How can I make the audience feel how I want them to feel?" Coaches acknowledge student experiences and allow them to inform the work, but never at the expense of audience understanding.

3. Everyone Acts in Ways That Meet Their Needs

Individuals in the group understand that no one acts against their own interests. The group solves problems, critiques ideas, and interacts with one another with the understanding that other people's lives are (at least partially) *knowable* by listening well and asking the right questions.

Disagreements can and should happen when examining human experiences. Those differing viewpoints need to occur without the unintentional valuing of one person's needs over another's. Finally, balance must be achieved between what is best for one individual and what is best for the team.

TEAM EXAMPLES: EVERYONE ACTS IN WAYS THAT MEET THEIR NEEDS

Poor/average teams: Player's fight to meet their own needs without regard for the group or anyone else. Other players' actions are incomprehensible or "wrong": It is obvious what is "right": Why can't everyone see it?

Good teams: Players unconsciously consider other's motivations, maybe because they like the group or respect some of its members. Players find it difficult to understand people that they do not like. Player's mostly do not intentionally address other's needs.

Excellent teams: Players intentionally address group's needs. Players ask questions and seek to understand where others are coming from. Players examine their own needs and can objectively compare them to the needs of the group and other players. Players seek to understand people with wildly different experiences than theirs, even people they do not respect or like.

4. Yes > No

Yes > No is an old improvisation rule. When someone mimes answering a phone and says, "It's for you," you take that phone. You don't say, "No it's not," or worse, "That's not a phone," or worse still, "You're crazy." The actor must say "Yes." Nothing shuts down a scene faster than saying "no" right after someone's made himself or herself vulnerable.

Yes > No means that individuals entertain new perspectives and ideas on many different levels, *physically* as well as intellectually. Individuals want to play and feel safe to fail—and succeed—spectacularly. The group accepts its individual members and their flaws.

Individuals feel comfortable committing to ideas that they don't understand (yet)—that will come with time. Action is the best way to understand anything. The default attitude of the group is generosity. Members of the group can laugh at themselves.

TEAM EXAMPLES: YES > NO

Poor/average teams: Players feel that the other players are laughing at them. Players resist making themselves vulnerable for fear of the group's judgment. Players do not act until they know exactly what they are doing. Players look for the "right way" and fear being "wrong." Coaches tell players what to do and discourage experimentation. Laughter comes at the expense of individuals.

Good teams: The group tends to talk for a long time before doing anything. Each member wants to know what everyone else is going to do so the group can be successful. Work often focuses on the boldest member of the group. Work comes out of discussion rather than play. Coaches ask for players' opinions and input, but player's worry they aren't giving the "right" answers, and sometimes the coach ignores their suggestions without trying them.

Excellent teams: Players want to put ideas on their feet right away. They are willing to enact ideas that they may or may not understand and are gracious when critiqued. They are willing to be uncomfortable around their group. There is a feeling of "If I succeed that's great, and if I fail, we all learn." Coaches decide what is more successful or less successful based on clear and explicit criteria and are willing to change course and consider especially good successes.

5. Everyone Owns Their Own Learning

Individuals claim ownership for their own learning process and journey. They have trust in themselves and make themselves trustworthy to others. They understand how to meet their own needs and work toward meeting the needs of others. They are willing/ready to be held accountable (trust issue).

This disposition requires an emotional bank account (Covey, 1989) with oneself and the willingness and ability to create emotional bank accounts with others. It requires a community perspective and the ability to see the bigger picture through reflection.

TEAM EXAMPLES: EVERYONE OWNS THEIR OWN LEARNING

Poor/average teams: Every player for himself. It is up to the coach or the captains to make sure that everyone does what he/she is supposed to do. There is little to no self-monitoring.

Good teams: They are committed to winning. Players work hard (sometimes even when the coach is not there) and the bonding between players is the shared pain and suffering that comes with the game.

Great teams: Individual players do what they need to do because they see team learning as their own learning. They support each other emotionally, intellectually, morally, physically, and socially—and at the same time hold each other accountable for excellence. They trust each other and are trusted by others.

6. Reflect and Revise

Individuals exhibit the ability to reconsider personal thoughts, beliefs, or actions in light of overwhelming evidence or in light of more powerful learning experiences. They have the ability to hold their current thoughts, beliefs, or actions as placeholders for something better rather than the one right absolute answer. They demonstrate the ability to play with ideas, thoughts, or perspectives without damage to their personal egos. They are curiosity driven.

This disposition emphasizes the ability to think reflectively, using evidence rather than mere perceptions. It is also creative in nature since rethinking requires a willingness to consider other ways of knowing (joyfully and intellectually).

TEAM EXAMPLES: BE FLEXIBLE OF THOUGHT

Poor/average teams: Players follow the rules others put before them. They see issues as right or wrong, black or white, fair or unfair. There is little to no attempt to understand the purpose of the rules. Since referees enforce the rules, they are viewed as the enemy.

Good teams: Play within the rules of the game and want everyone to follow the same rules. They appreciate good referees who hold everyone accountable to the same standards.

Great teams: Work to help everyone align their personal thoughts, beliefs, and actions with the evidence at hand. They are willing and able to play with ideas and alternatives and work toward balancing alternatives with "enough" evidence. Great teams do not need referees; they follow or recreate the rules as the evidence warrants (and to keep the game "fun").

7. Be Committed to the Team Learning Journey

One's motivation can be measured (yes really) by the amount of time, effort, and resources one spends on the learning task. Players who are committed see an alignment between their own personal learning and the learning goal of the team. They do what needs to be done because it meets their needs.

This disposition is evidenced through the ability to alter their personal or team learning goals, their ability to use "team learning" as the number one criteria for making individual and team decisions, providing appropriate support for others, and the willingness and ability to do the "right" things even when no one else is around to see it.

TEAM EXAMPLES: BE COMMITTED TO THE TEAM LEARNING JOURNEY

Average teams: Players are committed to their own learning journey. That personal learning may be at odds with what the team needs to be successful. Players may not see their own needs being met within the team structure/ team vision.

Good teams: There is a mix of players committed to team learning and others committed to their personal journeys. If the chances for success are good, players appear committed, when success is elusive, commitment fades.

Great teams: See their own success in the team experience (win or lose). They acknowledge other's contributions as essential and are committed to helping others whose individual learning goals do not align with the team's goals.

Choosing to "think like a thespian" is a dispositional issue. It means to think in certain ways, to value some experiences more than others, and have a willingness to reconsider everything. If beginning thespians play Brainball (TE) well, they learn a certain set of dispositions—a set of dispositions that they will use every single day of their lives.

Chapter Seven

Tip 2

Play the Game

One reason people choose to go out for school activities is because they want to have fun ("fun" defined as "appropriately challenging"). The trick to keeping things fun is to have enough information to get started but not enough to be overwhelmed or too little which leads to boredom (people shouldn't have to memorize an entire army of facts and skills before playing the game).

Games work because there are immediate, concrete consequences for every decision a player makes. Players actually get to "see" what happens for every decision they make—and that sets them up for powerful learning opportunities. It is clear when a particular strategy, skill, or disposition works (or doesn't). Those moments of failure (and success) become "teachable moments."

Teachable moments are when an individual is emotionally ready to learn something. They *want* to know an answer, a different way of doing something or would appreciate a new perspective. The very best teachers *plan* teachable moments—they know that within this five-minute span, students will ask this specific question!

Brainball (TE) and every good game is dynamic. The coach needs to be aware of how the game itself makes clear what the player needs to learn next. People learn by (a) doing and then (b) connecting their decisions to the consequences.

To become better at a game, the player needs to constantly evaluate which area he/she needs to improve upon: knowledge issues, skill issues, or disposition issues. The overall level of play is only as high as the weakest area. For example, people with a high level of knowledge and skill, but poor dispositions will be unable to play at a high level because they won't choose to act in ways that embrace individual and group learning.

Everyone has encountered teams like this. Teams that are skilled and knowledgeable but undisciplined or teams that know the game and play well as a team but just don't have the skills to get the job done. Luckily, when teams learn by doing, the next learning step is obvious. They just improve their weakest area until it isn't the weakest any more.

Knowledge issues, skill issues, and disposition issues all sound differently when they are the limiting factor in a team's performance. When knowledge issues limit a team, it sounds like "I don't know this," or "Why did that happen?" If skills are the problem, it sounds like "I need to learn to …" or "We need to practice …" These are typical questions for both teachers and coaches.

Disposition issues, though, are a little tricky. Dispositions come across as "What do I need to do to make this fun (appropriately challenging)?" That isn't a question teachers and coaches get all that often. It's a scary question for both students and teachers because it is connected on a deep level to the question, "Why do I need to know this?"

ATHLETICS VERSUS CLASSROOM

For traditional games, disposition questions are easier to answer. To an athlete who asks why they need to know something, a coach will answer, "Do you want to get better or not?" and the team will do what the coach needs to do because the coach wants to win. It's obvious and relevant to the coach.

Traditional games deal with dispositions very easily because they are based in competition, and not just any competition: We mean good competition. A good team competes against the other team. A great team competes against their own expectations (it is a deliberate learning journey).

All athletes want to excel/win. They join the sport because there is immediate feedback to their learning (practice). A good coach positions the other team as the opponent. A great coach will replace "winning" with "learning" as the ultimate goal and position "the opponent" as the measuring stick rather than "the enemy."

> *Ben's Story: My senior year in high school I was part of a soccer team that had many of the qualifications of a great team. When we finally lost at sectional finals (which ended our season), we all felt as though we'd lost more than the game. We'd played together for four years, and even though we weren't best friends (we didn't even all like each other), we'd grown, learned, succeeded, and failed together.*
>
> *A friend asked me, "I mean, it's just a game, right?"*
>
> *She was right of course; it is just a game, and it wasn't the first, nor most important game we'd ever lost. But it was our last game together—we'd become*

used to learning from our mistakes, and it was strange that we wouldn't be able to do that anymore: we'd lost the game, but we'd also lost a whole system of learning that we'd worked hard to create and sustain.

In classrooms, however, not all students *want* to excel/win: It just isn't a motivating factor for some students. Teachers can't always use the test or performance to convince them to improve, partly because tests have a long tradition of being inherently not fun, and because few teachers try to change that. Tests are perceived as not fun, so they appear to students as less and less fun, leaving a sort of competition that's too simple and too detached. Imagine a game (other than monopoly) that people play even though it isn't fun. It just doesn't make any sense.

LEARNING BY DOING

Learning is the point of Brainball (TE). Learning means a change in thoughts, behaviors, or beliefs. Players should become better—better people, better at examining and expressing their experiences through representative actions (thespians), and better community members.

Learning answers the question: "How else can this experience be expressed?" This model of learning is self-motivated. The need to learn isn't far off and abstract. Students need to learn because it meets their needs. Right here, and right now. An athlete will ask, "How do we overcome this particular opposing strategy?" and will demand and probably find answers. Classroom students should demand and find answers as well.

COMPETITION

Competition is how teams enact and measure what they've learned. Great teams use competition as a measuring stick for their own learning—that is, the opposing team represents a set of expectations to meet or overcome. When a team competes against a(n):

1. Average team (basic expectations): The chances for success are high. This allows teams to enact in real life, the pressured situations that they've been practicing and attempting to make a habit-of-mind (or body). Since it is low pressure, most players are relaxed, have time to think, and can process the game as it is taking place. Making theater and performing for the class would exemplify a basic expectation.
2. Good team (high/realistic expectations): The chances for success are more like 50/50. If the team performs its best, they may meet the expectation or

win. The risk is high but manageable and can be learningful with a good coach. To be successful, the players must implement all the knowledge, skills, and dispositions they've practiced. Making and performing for parents and the school would exemplify a high expectation.
3. Great team (highest expectations): The chances for success are slim (less than 50/50). They play against the odds, so they know what they have to learn next. It is (painfully sometimes) obvious which knowledge, skill, or disposition must be improved. For any hope of success, *everyone* has to play as a team and perform the best they have ever performed. Making, producing, and performing in community settings (auditions) would exemplify the highest expectation.

Playing against great teams (highest expectations) makes the abstract concrete. Teams see it, hear it, feel it, smell it, and taste it—the experience goes way beyond just what the coach thinks. Everyone now knows where he/she really stands as a team.

IN PRACTICE

Great coaches prepare for every learning cycle as if it were against a great team. They create the highest expectations as both personal and team visions.

Each game is made up of the rules and the field-appropriate knowledge, skills, and dispositions. The key to effective practice sessions is to construct the learning activities so as to make whatever issue is limiting improvement and growth obvious to the learner. An understanding of the basics of the game gives students the power to understand the basics' far-reaching implications.

By providing the basics and just enough information to propel them to the next learning issue, a good coach can create a "just-in-time" learning model (learning as it becomes relevant). Students who play the game are steering the ship, and overcoming challenges as they arise—what can be more relevant than that?

AUDIENCE

Many school "games" invite others to watch the students perform, whether it's a sport, a play, or a theater or dance concert. Audience matters to players. When players play the game, they are "performing," which means they wear certain clothes, act in certain ways, prepare to do their best, and feel maybe a little nervous (in a good way). They do this all because they'll be sharing their learning with people they care about—and that matters.

Through performances, theater naturally lends itself to this sharing with an audience. However, learning should not just be about performing well. When performing Brainball (TE), coaches need to invite parents, grandparents, administrators, teachers, and other students, and so on to see what their students have *learned* (this goes beyond just performing someone else's story or following someone else's directions). Expectations need to be clear and explicit, measured against prior learning (rather than each other), and wins (learning) celebrated!

A Brainball (TE) coach might include this information with a performance or host an "Informance" (informative performance) or "Open House" outside of the regular performances (at the end of a learning cycle). These shared *learning* performances include the context for the learning, the central concept they were investigating, process and community goals, and rubrics describing the product criteria. If possible, have students present and explain what they've learned to the various audience members.

Note: Remember it takes time (and multiple opportunities) to change a culture!

People join sports teams because they want to play the game for real, not just during practice sessions. Playing in front of real audiences makes their time, effort, and resources appear worthwhile. Play the game.

Chapter Eight

Tip 3

Competitions as Evaluations

How can a teacher tell if their students are learning? Traditionally in most content classrooms by taking a test at the end of the unit or semester. Tests work well if the teacher wants to measure knowledge, and performance tests for measuring skills, but Brainball (Theater Edition [TE]) is a disposition-centered model. Normal testing is just not going to fly.

A product like a test score is meaningless (as far as learning goes) if it isn't the result of a meaningful process. For great teams, winning the big game is only one indicator of what the team has learned, and acts as an indication of what the team needs to learn next. Brainball (TE) does the same thing; it de-emphasizes the performance and emphasizes the process and the community learning. This shift allows for a credible focus on the dispositions.

A big part of this shift is in how Brainball (TE) deals with assessments. In athletics, competitions are used to measure teams' learning and for Brainball (TE) assessments function in the same way. Assessments are deliberately inclusive of the process by which a product comes about, thereby testing more than just knowledge and skill.

EXAMPLE: INFORMANCE

It is 7:00 p.m. on a Tuesday night, the theater classroom is open, lights are on, and parents, students, and some school board members and administrators are entering the classroom. As they enter, everyone receives a criteria sheet and rubrics explaining the project requirements. You read that the project must include:

1. The problem statement linking a specific type of conflict to theater, the theatrical creation (through research, creating, experimenting, etc.), a

methodology identifying the learning process, and a one- to two-page conclusion with required terms highlighted.
2. The conclusion must use the required content words (list provided) to explain the creative process and outcome of their project.
3. They must list at least one contribution they made to the class or classmates *and* identify one contribution they received from a classmate (name, date, and specific contribution listed).
4. They must identify at least one thing they have "learned" through the project about:
   (a) themselves (this project focused on the disposition of "seeking beneficial solutions").
   (b) others (as team members and as individuals—at least one example of each).
   (c) theater (as a tool for life).

As you walk around the room viewing student performances (DVDs, YouTube, or scripts) you also notice that in each project (a) there is a completed scoring sheet (a summary of the teacher's evaluation and two classmates), and (b) a student response sheet where students talk about (i) how the classroom evaluation matched their perspective, (ii) how the project helped them meet their goals for themselves (goals listed), and (iii) what new learning goals they created for their next project.

ASSESSMENTS

First, assessments allow learners to "test themselves," to see what they have actually learned: Which area (knowledge, skill, or disposition) have they improved? During assessments, just like during soccer games, coaches are dispensable. Great coaches empower their players to create and play the game for themselves. By distancing themselves from the power structure, by acknowledging that everyone contributes something, great coaches allow students to experience learning that is meaningful to each individual.

Afterward, the player must reflect. Players don't learn anything from experiences until they process them (Dewey, 1938). It is during this time that they get to decide what knowledge, skill, or dispositional issues they need to improve next. If coaches do not give their students the opportunity to process and learn from their assessments, they are telling them that the scores or the performances are more important than the learning. Coaches should never give more weight to the product than the process, and in the case of Brainball (TE) the community aspect as well.

A well designed assessment creates a new "current reality," a new beginning point for the next learning cycle. Just like a team that has to deal with the next opposing team, Brainballers (ha ha) are continuously met with new goals and objectives against which to test themselves.

Assessments also show an external audience that learning has taken place. Students should feel comfortable performing in front of people and be excited to show what they are working on and learning together. The goal of an assessment is not to pass or fail students but to collect student-learning data.

Assessments in Brainball (TE) are both individual and team focused. A team that supports each member elevates its level of play on the whole. Great teams are not about their super stars (these players will always accomplish their goals) but about elevating the performance of the team as a whole. Teams should have high expectations of themselves so that wins are meaningful and should allow everyone the opportunity to contribute.

These factors make up the basics of an assessment. They are deliberately loose so they can apply to many different situations and teams. All assessments need to possess those qualities if they are to be effective. Here are some specific criteria for judging the actual quality of Brainball (TE) play:

1. Content knowledge (product)
   - Content facts (terminology) are identified and correct.
   - Correct terminology is used to explain the central concepts.
   - The terms lead to insights and interconnections (the learner puts the pieces together in meaningful ways).
   - Knowledge is being created by the learner (metacognition—they are aware that they are "learning").
   - Misconceptions are addressed (and relearned).
   - Content knowledge builds upon prior knowledge and serves as the foundation for the next learning cycle.
2. Process knowledge and skills
   - Skill usage at each step is developmentally appropriate and grows in sophistication.
   - The game flows through and with the parts—thinking leads from one step to another.
   - Steps are flexible/applicable to the question at hand.
   - Methodology is robust (appropriate for the question).
   - Conclusions are deep and robust (connected to the content).
   - More questions are generated than answered.
   - Thinking/acting/talking like a thespian emerges.
3. Community knowledge (team learning)
   - Alignment occurs between personal learning goals and team learning goals.

- Ability to merge personal needs with needs of the whole occurs.
- Synergy becomes "commonplace" in the classroom.
- Diversity is viewed as a strength of the group.
4. Relationship building and nurturing skills
    - Individuals take time, effort, and resources to learn about their classmates.
    - Individuals reference other's individual strengths and contributions.
    - Individuals develop emotional bank accounts with everyone in the class.
5. Disposition evidence (rubrics in chapter 6)
    - I am creative and so are you (how else?)
    - Audience mindset
    - Everyone acts in ways that meet their needs
    - Yes > No
    - Everyone owns their own learning
    - Reflection and revision
    - Be committed to the team learning journey

When coaching a team sport like Brainball (TE), every practice and assessment tells the coach (and players) what the group needs to work on next. It is the coach's responsibility to share that information with their team and to provide the team with the appropriate experiences to keep improving.

The coach needs to give them time to observe and reflect seriously on what things need fixing and then to create the next learning cycle to address that need. It is the coach's responsibility then to structure practices with that specific thing in mind. If a team needs to work on passing, the coach should use evidence (student-learning data) to explain why, and structure the proper exercises. If students need to work portraying a particular emotion, work on portraying that emotion instead of just moving on to the next scene.

All practices and games are formative until the end of the year when it becomes "win or go home." It is a learning process, not just a product. It doesn't end.

To play Brainball (TE) at the "Great" level, a coach must know what the next level of expertise looks like and what work is developmentally appropriate for the group. A coach needs to know what their group can handle and that there are *always* ways and things to improve. Preparing players for the next level while understanding where they are (at the moment) keeps the game fresh and interesting.

Chapter Nine

Tip 4

Sequences Matter

One size does not fit all when it comes to learning. Students will learn what they choose to learn. Every student's learning journey is unique because each student is unique.

This does not mean that classroom planning should be left to chance. Structuring lessons and units according to the proper sequences is important. Each person's learning is unique, not random. It is the coach's job to present the players with experiences that they learn from—those experiences are not random but rely on a set of sequences.

Coaches also need to match how they organize instruction to the ways their students organize information. Instruction that isn't based on and engendered by the student isn't instruction—it's presenting information.

Brainball (Theater Edition [TE]) structures the students' experiences using three different sets of sequences: lesson plans, the steps of inquiry (process), and community building. Each sequence is modified to teach one of the central concepts of theater, dependent upon the prior experiences of the students and their developmental needs at that moment.

LESSON PLAN STRUCTURE

Brainball (TE) uses the 5Es Learning Cycle Lesson Plan (Bybee, 2015) format to structure the daily lesson plans in section 3. The 5Es stand for:

1. Engage. Invite students into the learning episode, clarify today's learning task, and remind them of what they have already learned.
2. Explore. Have them access (in small groups) what they think they already know (this happens before you share any content information) or have

them experience some hands-on item or examples (directly connected to what you will be talking about later).
3. Explain. Describe how the field views the knowledge, skill, or disposition (the lecture portion of the lesson). Explain the explore activity in theater terms.
4. Elaborate. Have the students *use* the new knowledge, skill, or disposition (they practice).
5. Evaluate. While it is listed last, evaluation really takes place in every step (track their learning progress against your goal for the day).

The 5Es are cyclical by design. The end of a learning cycle should beget a new learning cycle ("Well, if that was true for x, could it be true for y?"). Students should be encouraged to go from the end of one lesson to the beginning of the next lesson. Units are when all the days are connected to teach one central concept (the days together as a sequence mirror process learning in theater).

Think of a soccer coach who wants to work on defensive positioning. For a soccer practice, the 5Es might take the form of warm-ups (engage), doing some small two-on-one or two-on-two games (explore), set positions and give objectives, point out weaknesses or areas of improvement (explain), play full field (elaborate), and watch and fix, reposition players (evaluate).

UNIT PLAN STRUCTURE (PROCESS): THEATER INQUIRY

Most students are not taught a theater inquiry sequence. Theater inquiry is defined as "the asking and answering of theatrical questions in theatrically appropriate ways." Generally speaking, students are taught the things they need in order to perform well. Theater inquiry includes the examination of a human experience and then the efforts to express those experiences through representative actions.

The examination of the human experience is metacognition in action, teaching students to reflect upon their lives and themselves (an important component of becoming self-actualized). Donald Schon talks about two forms of reflections: (a) reflection-in-action and (b) reflection-on-action. We would like to add a third: (c) reflection-on-self.

1. Reflection-in-action asks, "What were you thinking during that human experience?"
2. Reflection-on-action asks, "How did you think about that experience afterwards?"
3. Reflection-on-self asks, "What do your thoughts, ideas, and questions tell you about *your* beliefs, values, and prior experiences?"

Students come to school with all sorts of life experiences (some of which are truly hard to comprehend). They have questions: about things that worry and stress them, thoughts, and questions about themselves and others, how to deal with conflict, how to cope with both loving and hating themselves, how is it possible to feel both superior and almost worthless. They need help processing those human thoughts.

Students also need help expressing those thoughts/experiences using representative actions. Theater is a powerful learning opportunity because it allows students to "play out" different roles, different endings, and different strategies—all in a safe and learningful environment. It allows them to "try-on" a different persona without trampling their own sense of self. It is magical—the ability to explore different ways of viewing life with little risk. Thus, the importance of theater—for everyone!

Theatrical inquiry is about asking human-focused questions and attempting to answer them in theatrically appropriate ways. A set of steps for theater inquiry is:

1. Observation
2. Curiosity
3. Problem statements

The three steps listed above focus on studying the human experience in question. The following seven steps are specific to theater inquiry:

1. Gathering information
2. Plan
3. Compose (first draft)
4. Evaluate
5. Revise
6. Edit
7. Submit/perform

The last two steps focus on debriefing the entire learning process—what was accomplished and what did we learn?

1. Analysis
2. Conclusions

Unit plans focus on one central concept at a time and allow students to take a basic idea, connect it to what they already know, and see more complexities in that concept. This works because games (theater inquiry) have replay value. One becomes better at a game by playing it and then thinking about it. Games become more complex the longer one plays (if it remains relevant).

When coaches plan lessons with the steps of theater inquiry in mind, students experience a clear series of steps for thinking, for asking questions, for attempting to answer them in a logical way, and for communicating their results to a wider audience.

The sequence for theater inquiry is the vocabulary with which thespians communicate. It is pure "theater." Thespians need to communicate using the same common language. Rather than picking up a script and simply learning it, a great team of thespians uses and communicates through steps of inquiry to explore the human experience and ways to express it, create the script, and perform the invented piece. Learning to ask and answer questions is a powerful tool, but only if students see that it is a relevant skill. Otherwise, it stays in the classroom.

COMMUNITY BUILDING STRUCTURE: THE THEATER COMMUNITY

Since Brainball (TE) is a team sport (and all teams would rather be great than average or good), a coach's classroom must learn to function like a community. The third planning sequence deals with the transformation of the classroom (a group of individuals) into a team (a community). The community-building sequence is similar to the steps of individual learning journeys such as those made explicit in Brown and Moffet's *The Hero's Journey* (chapter 1). There are two models that explain the community-building sequence (Tuckman, 1965; Egolf, 2001):

Model 1 (Tuckman)/Model 2 (Egolf)

1. Pseudo community/forming: The group works together but has reservations about the usefulness of the group. They appear to agree verbally and visually with one another while secretly disagreeing.
2. Chaos/storming: The group begins to disagree with one another outwardly. Differences are shared (which is uncomfortable).
3. Emptying/norming: The group begins to view differences as strengths and use individual strengths to accomplish common goals.
4. True community/performing: Each member of the group contributes from an area of personal strength. The atmosphere is supportive and respective. Mutual goals are established and individual goals and growth are supported.

Building communities from a group of individuals is complex, more complex than content learning because it includes multiple individuals with their own thoughts, beliefs, and changing needs. Individual knowledge is hard to teach.

The Five Dysfunctions of a Team (Lencioni, 2002) describes the change in relationships that occur if people move through the stages (a sequence) toward true community. They include: building trust, addressing conflict, fostering commitment to the shared vision, holding one another accountable, and a focus on results.

TRUST

Trust is a quality-of-life issue and is the foundation of all meaningful relationships. In a natural group, people trust that they have something in common with other members of the group, even if it's unclear what that is, because everyone has made the decision to be there.

Because membership in natural groups is voluntary, a positive spiral ensues: A student chooses to be a part of the group, and so the group meets their needs, which leads them to continue to be part of the group and so on. They work hard at the group because it meets their needs, and it meets their needs because they work hard, and they trust that all members of the group are alike in this aspect, even if they are alike in nothing else.

Merriam-Webster defines "trust" as "reliance on the integrity, strength, ability, surety, of a person or a thing; confidence." While technically correct, it might be more useful to consider in what ways trust manifests in everyday relationships. A trustworthy or trusting person will:

1. Keep their word without reminders or nagging.
2. Admit weaknesses and mistakes (not as excuses, but as limiters).
3. Ask for help when they need it.
4. Accept questions and input about their accepted responsibilities.
5. Believe that a mistake is a mistake, and that everyone is doing the best he/she can.
6. Give assistance and feedback (take the risk), and provide information versus advice.
7. Offer and accept apologies (and let it go).

Remember, it's the coach's responsibility to do two things: model and label the steps of community building (make them explicit). The coach must trust, be worthy of trust (model those behaviors), and address issues of trust explicitly in class (label issues as they arise).

Trust describes relationships. Since teams are made up of individuals, the coach's relationship with their team is just the sum of the relationships they have made with each individual member of the team. A good team doesn't become a great team until there's a great level of trust between all members of the team.

This would be a good time to note that trust is developmental in nature. Sean Covey describes trust as the balance of a bank account. A bank account isn't black and white, money or no money, but rather something, that needs to be maintained and paid attention to.

Just like a financial bank account, an emotional bank account can have a positive balance (good) or a negative balance (not good). Covey lists six ways to make deposits into one's emotional bank account:

1. Understand the individual (what's important to them).
2. Attend to the little things (little acts of kindness).
3. Keep commitments (promises).
4. Clarify expectations.
5. Show personal integrity (loyalty—to those not present, treat others as you would like to be treated).
6. Apologize sincerely when making a withdrawal (forgiveness rather than sorry).

Withdrawals from the emotional bank account might look like: betraying trust (i.e., discourtesy, disrespect, overreacting, not listening, ignoring others, being arbitrary, or holding power over others).

CONFLICT

When teams trust their teammates, they see multiple, constructive ways to deal with conflict. Constructive conflict is based in trust. The inner dialogue of each person in the group closely resembles the outer dialogue. That means that people say what they think. Furthermore, with constructive conflict, direct dialogue is the best way to fulfill the needs of both the team and the individual.

Because the health of the team and the health of the individual are so closely tied together, teams are able to draw on a multiplicity of ideas and experiences without feeling as though they are devalued by others. By valuing the experiences of all team members, they themselves are valued.

A great team will have few political spats. Poor group politics occur when it is more important that I (rather than you, or Sarah, or Max) have an idea, rather than whether the idea has any merit. Those are personality conflicts (who has the power, and who is right or wrong). Success comes at the expense of or in despite of the group.

Great teams never consider the "who" more important than the "what." They talk about topics, not trivia. They are objective and focused.

This does not mean that teams are free of conflict. Teams have productive conflict. Productive conflict deals with concepts and ideas that concern the entire team (such as getting the best solution in the shortest amount of time).

Teamwork and community maintenance are not easy. Teams aren't magical and do not always get along. Teams are made up of people, and people are flawed. Having access to multiple perspectives does not mean easier. It does, however, improve the probability of a generative long-term solution.

Teamwork is often uncomfortable, especially in the beginning when the team is first learning what it means to trust and forgive (and be forgiven) by their teammates. It takes time and work to become a team.

For example, imagine how a team in the "Pseudo/Forming" stage would react to someone who says what they think and mean ("I think there might be a better way to go about this"). In the beginning stage, even though the behavior (saying what one thinks) is appropriate and necessary for the team, it doesn't come naturally, and people will have negative reactions.

In fact, it would be considered at that moment as a withdrawal from one's emotional bank account. Any conflict before a team becomes a team is going to appear as a withdrawal; no one in a group of individuals likes to be disagreed with.

But it is a necessary (and required) risk for a team. If individuals do not say what they mean, they are showing that they have little trust in the rest of the group.

So instead, think about beginning a conflict as taking out a loan. Members will be able to repay the group when they become a team. A team will see disagreements as a pathway to new solutions.

As a team matures and begins to build trust, it will begin to seek Win–Win solutions. Win–Win solutions are much more difficult to achieve than Win–Lose (the norm). Voting is an example of Win–Lose, where the loser has little obligation to the winner. Lose–Lose is another option, where a consensus is reached and no one gets what he or she really wants. A team that seeks Win–Win solutions knows that everyone is good at something and will draw on everyone's strengths and perspectives.

When the team starts to consider Win–Win situations rather than Win–Lose, that initial withdrawal will come back around in the form of a deposit. That is what sets the precedence for a healthy team.

COMMITMENT

Great teams need to be structured in a way so that acting in the interest of the team meets individual needs as well. Having an explicit learning goal (a shared vision for the learning journey) helps to align individual and group needs, thereby making it easier for individuals to commit to the journey.

There are several factors coaches should consider as their teams are picking a vision.

First of all, a team vision will need to meet individual needs (safety, freedom, power, fun, love, and belonging). This will make the vision relevant. A relevant vision will help people want to change more than they want to stay the same. If a vision isn't relevant, there isn't a connection between the good of the individual and the good of the team, and people will continue to act in ways that only meet their individual needs.

Second, a team vision should create a sense of commonality. It will give the group a common vocabulary and will lend coherence to diverse activities and experiences. A shared vision will make students feel as though they are united in an important undertaking (which they are). A shared vision allows people to be "a part of something important," which is a deep need indeed.

Shared visions provide focus and energy for learning. They foster and encourage educated risk-taking and play. Bold actions, when firmly rooted in the good of the team, are heroic, rather than distracting. It is exciting and inspiring to watch someone try something entirely new when it could improve the fare of an entire team (and one's own self). It inspires a person to "do what needs to be done," which inspires others to think and act courageously.

Commitment means that one's own personal vision is the team's vision. Commitment, however, isn't the only choice students have when subscribing to a vision. According to Peter Senge, they might instead be enrolled, compliant, apathetic, or noncompliant.

- Enrolled: Students want the team vision.
- Compliant: Students do what others ask even if it isn't their vision.
- Apathetic: Students don't care enough to get in the way.
- Noncompliant: Students actively work to stop the team's movement toward the goal.

Imagine the outline of a big arrow pointing to the right. The big arrow represents the team vision or the good of the team. Inside the big arrow are many smaller arrows, pointing in many different directions. The small arrows represent the goals of individuals.

The small arrows that point the same direction as the big arrow are committed, the ones pointing the opposite direction noncompliant. How closely the small arrows align to the big arrow describes the overall level of "commitment" of the team members. On a great team, all the small arrows will generally point the same direction as the big arrow.

Small arrow and big arrow alignment means that everyone believes that the team has everyone's best interests at heart and that the group shares a common aspiration.

Teams that are committed to the shared vision are remarkable organizations. A committed team will appear to have certain traits to outsiders. They will have a clear direction and priorities and will focus on objectives rather than trivia. The mistakes of individual team members are quickly absorbed, intellectualized, and learned from by the whole team. The team moves forward without hesitation and acknowledges mistakes without guilt.

ACCOUNTABILITY

Unlike many organizations, teams have to formally hold each other accountable. Rather than grumbling about coworkers behind their backs or simply phasing them out of the group as a nonentity, the success of a team is based on the success of the individuals; if one team member fails, the team fails.

An effective working relationship will ensure that poor performers feel pressure to perform, but in a supportive rather than hostile way. If the team says what it thinks rather than grumbling or complaining on the sly, the relationship between the team and the individual will be obvious, and the poor performer will understand that their success is important to the success of the team. This doesn't happen by itself, but is an action that the team takes.

If an individual feels that they are accountable to the rest of the team, the team is accountable to them, and everyone is accountable to the standards of success set forth in the team vision, everyone is able to avoid the bureaucracy that surrounds performance and corrective action. They know that they are all held up to the same high standards.

With that objectivity, the team is able to quickly identify problems by questioning assumptions without hesitation, without taking it personally, for the good of the team.

It is the team's responsibility to find the role that each individual is able to play (how each person is able to contribute) and help that person's contributions to be as strong as possible. This makes contributions a public thing and brings "what he says" and "what she does" closer together. It allows the rest of the team to learn from the individual's learning and puts supportive pressure on others to display their own learning.

Learning as a team and as an individual is a cycle: practice, perform, review, revise ... practice perform, review, revise. Repeat (over and over again). Each stage of the cycle informs the next stage of the cycle and makes permanent the previous stage.

But it won't just happen by itself. It is a decision. Teams can't just *think* about it, they have to *do* it.

FOCUS ON RESULTS

Many of the traits of a great team are simply derivatives of this simple theme: Results (facts) are more important than perception. Clear communication is fact based. Keeping one's word is factual. Trust is factual. Rubrics are factual. Team visions are based on facts. With established facts, there's a reality to agree or disagree with.

Facts are not political; they are concrete and measurable. For athletics, we measure the success of the team by the facts: Did the team win or lose? How long did we possess the ball? What did the team learn? In the classroom, rubrics and the team vision measure success.

When the measurement of success is based on facts (rubrics, clear communication, the team vision), the next step is also based on facts: "If x is where we fell short, then x is obviously where we need to spend more resources improving." Coaches and students can ask, "Did it work?" and not only is the answer real and true but also provides direction for the next learning step.

Facts are the results of intentional inquiry. Teams that focus on results retain and improve players. Results-based teams understand how successful or unsuccessful they have been and respond in kind.

Perhaps most importantly, teams that focus on facts avoid distractions. They "beg the question" as a matter of course and habit, asking, "Is this relevant?" or "Does this align with the team vision?" They see politics as an unwelcome distraction from the team vision.

LEARNING SEQUENCES

Sequence matters for the intellectual, social, emotional, physical, and moral needs of your students. Following a series of scripts is a sequence that focuses on covering material rather than individual and team "learning."

Being "developmentally appropriate" means to begin where the students are, not where the coach wishes they would be. A proper sequence takes them from where they are (at that time and place) and moves them toward where they need to be in order to grow into self-actualized human beings.

There is a time and place for topics, concepts, issues, thinking in specific ways, information, and skills development. Just because the coach is ready to address something doesn't mean it is best for the student.

Appropriate sequences have everything to do with teacher (coach) expectations. It is up to the coach to provide the "right" experience so students/players can have enough success to keep them interested, along with enough failures to show them what they still have to learn. A delicate balance indeed!

Learning sequences are a "risk-management" system. They have risk (that's what makes the games fun), but the failures are learning oriented rather than emotional failures.

Good planning increases (not guarantees) the chances for success (and that means learning). That means planning for different students, different classes, and different content foci. Planning is about probability—good planning means more students will learn more (content, process, and a community orientation).

Learning sequences include the daily plans (5Es), unit plans (process—central concept focused), and community building. This multitiered approach allows coaches to connect every day's learning to what matters most—students' lives outside the classroom setting.

Chapter Ten

Tip 5

Explicit Communications

In Brainball (Theater Edition [TE]) *doing* the discipline and making it relevant go hand in hand. If students can't *do* it, they can't process it, mess with it, pattern and plot it, and learn from it. Students experience what they do. They memorize what they can't do.

And learning comes from processing the experience. John Dewey (1938) says, "You do not learn from experience, you learn from processing the experience!" Both the National Learning Council (2000) and Darling-Hammond (2008) say that providing time to reflect on experiences is a key component of personal learning. Even though classes will experience the same things, individuals within that class will learn different things from those experiences. Talking about the different ways people experience events allows for a shared experience to become "learningful."

When good things happen (product, process, or community), people do one of two things. They either write it off as a stroke of luck or they ask why. They might look at the circumstances and decide that it really was just a stroke of luck, but they might also find that the good thing was the result of something replicable.

CLASS STRUCTURE

Brainball (TE) is a classroom system wherein transparency and making the "common sense" explicit is a central strength. It is the teacher's responsibility to do two things:

1. Model the behavior and learning they expect from their students, and
2. Label the behavior and learning they model.

Explicit communication means to acknowledge the failures and struggles as well as the successes of the group. Make explicit the structure of the game. Students win the game by learning, not by passing a test. They are not competing with one another; rather, there is enough success to go around (that means for everyone). Teachers also need to acknowledge their own successes and failures. As part of the team, they need to ask students' questions, listen to the answers, and try out their ideas. Coach and students together learn from one another's diverse experiences.

Coaches need to talk about relevance issues (why is this important and worth learning), self-actualization and the needs of their students, their individual strengths and weaknesses, and growth.

Coaches also need to explicitly connect learning to their students' needs (fun, freedom, power, love, and belonging to name a few). No one acts in ways that don't fulfill one's needs, so coaches need to make the connection between classroom learning and "real life" obvious. Coaches need to talk about relationships, about frustration—all the experiences we have that make us human. Coaches cannot be afraid to be passionate and make themselves vulnerable. Theater as a discipline is relevant to the coach; it has helped put life into perspective. Coaches need to talk about that.

To model the game effectively, coaches need to make their thinking evident all the time (Think-Aloud is a great Brainball [TE] strategy). Coaches must think about their own thinking and talk about it with their students. When a coach does this, they have encouraged their students to the same. They have modeled and labeled how to be metacognizant.

At some point in the learning journey, the hero (student) has to know what he or she is fighting for. Heroes have an explicit goal to accomplish. Frodo grows into and directs his learning journey by understanding that the Ring of Power must be destroyed, Harry Potter that he must vanquish Lord Voldemort. Everything about their journeys are structured to this explicit purpose (the end-in-mind).

If the coach doesn't make explicit what they and the students are fighting for, how can they expect them to be committed? An average team has a vague sense of purpose; a great team knows exactly where the journey is going.

Making the end-in-mind explicit is helpful so that the coaches can position them as fellow learners. They can give students permission to codesign the experiences that are relevant to them, create their own knowledge, and allow them to participate wholeheartedly in the improvement of their own lives.

TALKING ABOUT PRODUCT

1. Coaches need to talk about content understanding: They need to name and explain content facts and central concepts. Facts and concepts are the

language of the field (just not the only thing). Content facts are the byproduct of doing the process, not the number one outcome.

> *Mickey's Story: When I was getting my Master's in Biology, my Stats teacher had written the book we were using (he was kind of smart). All our exams were open book and open notes and here was his rationale: When you are a professional researcher, you will want to use the right formula for the right information, and that means that you will look it up—at first.*
>
> *After looking it up enough times, it will be to your advantage (it will meet your needs) to memorize that formula. For now, it is more important to know which tool works best for the job at hand.*
>
> *I have never forgotten his words—and that was before the days of technology!*

Relevant content is the result of the learning process, not the learning process itself. Facts matter when they are the result of one's own learning. Students remember facts only insofar as they are relevant.

2. Talk about connections to prior learning: Connecting current learning to prior knowledge (identifying the central concept and connecting them to their prior learning experiences) helps students place their knowledge in the "big picture." Connecting to what they already know simplifies the learning process and gives them added confidence.

Explicitly spiraling learning also helps the brain organize the new facts into a well-developed concept. Talking about the same central concept over and over again provides opportunities to rethink what they know and put those ideas into their long-term memory. It also allows them the opportunity to appreciate the complexity of powerful ideas (the more you know, the less you know).

3. Let students talk: Audience provides outside eyes for their learning (parents, grandparents, other teachers and students, the rest of the theater community, or maybe even taxpayers). An outside audience further cements the idea of "students versus the game."

Furthermore, it shows that the work the community is doing is important and worth showing to people. If students believe, something is important (relevant), they deserve the opportunity to show it to a wider audience, just as they have with the smaller theater community of the classroom.

Finally, talking about their content learning with others gives them one last opportunity to put those facts into their long-term memory.

TALKING ABOUT PROCESS

1. Coaches need to let students talk during lessons: One key finding about learning (supported by both Darling-Hammond and the National Learning

Council) is that students should talk first. Coaches should allow students to react, predict, define, draw, and describe; alone first and then in groups. Students know a lot already—the coach should find out what the students know (and what they think they know) before they share content knowledge, conceptual understandings, or facts. Letting students talk before the coach (the explore of the lesson) establishes community and communication as essential parts of the game.

Note: Again, the coach must *tell* the students that community and communication are essential parts of the game. If students never talk about it, they will never learn that a community of learners can be *built* rather than merely experienced through serendipity.

Everyone experiences the world subjectively. They are all individuals who possess their own knowledge, belief systems, and dispositions. Just because everyone has shared the same experiences does not mean that everyone's learned the same things.

Coaches should not make the students figure out what they were supposed to have learned by themselves. Instead, they need to provoke a group discussion and talk about what kind of experiences they have "shared." Coaches must ask students to think about it, change perspectives for a moment, and ponder "what ifs." Intellectual play is about options and alternatives rather than the search for the one right answer.

And if the coach never talks about it, they have no way of knowing or gauging the learning that hopefully took place. If they do not ask, how can they know what their students have learned through the theatrical process?

And then they should talk about *that*. Why did they experience that in the way they did? What went right or wrong? Why did they do it? What decisions were made, and what were the consequences of those decisions? It is not enough to think—they should ask their students why they thought what they thought.

2. Coaches need to talk about diversity (of thoughts, beliefs, and actions): When a coach models and talks about creativity (seeing things from different perspectives) and contributions as important to the team, they are defining the way the community goes about its work—the process of learning.

The coach needs to make the process both explicit and important (by talking about it repeatedly). Students are living in a consumer world where having what everyone else has (in their views) makes them special (and yes, we think that is oxymoronic too). Coaches have to show them that great teams rely on people being different and bringing their unique strengths to the group.

Diversity matters to the players if it matters to their coach.

3. Coaches need to talk about development: Since developmental changes are a biological process, coaches need to talk with students about their changing needs (and thoughts and emotions and so on). How their bodies, minds, thinking, emotions, friends, and ideas of right and wrong are changing as they grow.

Many students think, "I am the only one who feels, thinks, or believes this way." Since most adults do not talk about these students' changing needs, students are left to fend for themselves. Making those changes "normal" meets the needs of the students (and allows them to focus their energies on the learning you have planned).

TALKING ABOUT COMMUNITY: WHEN 1 + 1 + 1 = 5

There are plenty of situations where an individual can be more effective than a group (it worked for James Bond anyway). But the students are not foiling Dr. Evil (yet); they are trooping to theater class with a bunch of people they know almost nothing about. They aren't lone wolves when they are in a room with a bunch of their peers, no matter how hard they try. In groups, lone wolves don't exist. They are either a collection of individuals or a team.

And a team is almost always better than a collection of individuals: It can accomplish more, satisfy more needs, and solve bigger problems than a collection of individuals.

But why? How does the total worth of a group equal more than the sum of the group's parts? How does 1 + 1 + 1 = 5?

Brainball (TE) deals with a classroom of humans, not numbers. Humans are far better than numbers (if given the chance). Humans are both illogically good and illogically bad, which numbers will never be able to do.

So really, the real question is not *how* 1 + 1 + 1 = 5, but rather *when*, and what coaches can do to ensure that their equation comes out 1 + 1 + 1 = 5, rather than 1 + 1 + 1 = 3, or worse, 1 + 1 + 1 = 2 (everyone's been a part of that group at one time or another).

This idea of a group being more than a collection of individuals is commonly called "synergy," though usually organizations stop somewhere in between talking about it and doing it.

"Synergy" is defined by *Merriam-Webster* as "a mutually advantageous compatibility of participants" and synergism as "the total effect is greater than the sum of the individual effects."

Great teams use their people in ways that lead to synergy. Each individual benefits more from being a team member than by being part of a group of individuals. They learn more, contribute more, and play a role in team success.

Those types of relationships do not happen overnight and must be made explicit—if the learning and experience is to go beyond "luck."

1. Coaches need to talk about the stages of building community: The stages of building community must be made explicit. Naming the stages helps everyone understand that those steps are in fact "normal." It is "normal" to play nice, to be in chaos, to share views that are unique (and different from others), and to grow into being a functional part of a team. Those stages are "normal," not easy.

> *Mickey's Story: When I was a senior in college I took a course entitled: Thanatology—The Study of Death and Dying. My friends wondered about that choice and I always said "Everyone I know is probably going to die; I think I should know something about it."*
>
> *Less than a year later, my Dad died. Since we had studied Elisabeth Kubla-Ross's work, I could name the stage I was going through in my grieving process. It didn't make it easier, it made it human and "normal." And that also meant I knew that someday, I would get through it.*

Growing (and labeling) through community-growing stages helps students move beyond the one experience to the next learning opportunity. They are prepared for life rather than just prepared for school.

2. Coaches need to talk about relationships/contributions: Since Brainball (TE) takes place in a community, where members of the group learn from each other, the coach must communicate about community learning as well. It can't stay up in the coach's head; they have to share it. True communities are strong because people pool their personal realizations and thoughts to create something more powerful than the "one."

By making community an explicit goal (something students devote their time and energy into developing), coaches can provide a platform for acknowledging diversity and, therefore, different ways of thinking and perceiving reality.

The coach must talk to them about where they are going. That includes what knowledge, skills, and dispositions make up a great team and what end they will be working toward. It includes the developmental trajectory of the game; what concepts will they be learning next, as well as what the next step is. And it includes talking about the qualities that high-functioning communities tend to possess, like verbal and active listening skills.

Finally, coaches must talk about the interpersonal skills that make a community successful, such as dealing with conflict effectively, trusting one another, holding each other accountable, and getting results. Without talking about any of this, coaches attribute anything good that these students make or learn to simple, dumb luck.

Section Three

DAY-TO-DAY LESSON PLANS
Brainball Illuminated

Since some readers will begin here (we really know you theater teachers)—hello! Section 3 is made up of actual lesson plan examples, which are (hopefully) no more and no less than the *doing* of the theories in sections 1 and 2. If the reader should have any "I wonder what they are talking about?" or "Why did they organize things in that way?" questions as they use this section, they are probably answered in the first two sections.

This section provides daily lesson plans formatted in a 5Es model that teaches process, product, and community. The individual lesson plans and the mapped-out sequence have been designed and tested to work in a 45-minute class period.

These daily plans are not "teacher-proof." They require the teacher's knowledge, skills, and dispositions (willingness to take a risk in the hopes of something more meaningful). The more the teacher knows, the more experiences he or she has with the plans and the sequence, and the more interesting and effective the plans become.

For many teachers, the first time through is the hardest. Few teachers have had multiple theater courses that modeled this type of inquiry and community learning—nor do most university methods courses make these steps explicit. That means relearning how and what to teach everyday—and that's challenging (the teacher's own personal learning journey).

It is tempting to stick with what one knows, insert activities that will work, and pick and choose the most comfortable lessons. The lessons described here, however, are designed to build off each other (they are scaffolded) and emphasize product (theater content), process (theater inquiry), and community (working effectively with others). The closer a teacher can stick to the daily plans (the first time through), the more success they will have in all three areas. Once they have been through the sequence, modifying the plans to better meet their students' and their own needs becomes normal (SCAMPER; Eberle, 2008; appendix 2).

These plans can (and are supposed to) be modified for any audience from fifth through twelfth grade. They are meant to mirror a "learning-on-demand" model of learning, where students will need "just enough information" to continue the learning process. That requires a delicate balance between too much (boring) and not enough (frustrating) information. Fortunately, today's students have many experiences with this type of learning (imagine any electronic game where they play until they are "killed" and then play again using just a little more information).

A couple of quick notes:

Key ideas behind the 5Es Learning Cycle lesson plans include:

1. Engage them with a real life story or example—catch their interest before beginning the lesson. Making the lesson relevant goes here.
2. Students do some sort of small group task (Explore) before any "teaching" happens; define a term, experience some real items (role play, small scene, facial expressions, etc.). Students should access what they think they already know here.
3. Then the "teaching" (Explain). Teachers should use whatever format works (interactive lecture, lecture, PowerPoint, etc.) for them. When the teacher can connect their lecture to their students' thoughts (Explore) this part is more interactive.
4. Students practice *doing* the task that meets the teacher's learning outcome (Elaborate).
5. The coach evaluates throughout to make sure learning is on the right path (Explore, Explain, and Elaborate).

The actual student learning occurs when they share their experiences and the teacher puts the learning concept into theater terms!

Lessons 1–3 teaches them how to make observations. Lesson 4 helps students reengage their curiosity while lesson 5 focuses student curiosity into something worth studying (problem statements). Lessons 6–11 focus on helping students grasp essential theater information (voice, space, scripts, costumes, set design, and feedback). Lessons 12–20 help students create their own performances through planning, picking, composing reviewing, revising, constructing, and then testing. Lessons 21 and 22 are the performances—first in-class and then for an external audience. Lesson 22 focuses on analyzing the entire inquiry process and finally lesson 23 helps students synthesize what they have actually learned (conclusion).

Section 3 provides a framework for making theater relevant to students. The teacher owns the activities with their own examples, activities, and connections to the lives of their specific audience. How it actually looks in two years will be unique. You teach who you are! Enjoy the journey.

Chapter Eleven

Lesson Plans

LESSON 1: OBSERVATIONS: FITTING IN

Student learning goals: Students will practice the skill of observation for use both inside and outside the classroom.

Engage: The goal is for students to begin thinking about what "fitting in" means. (5 minutes)

Introduce students to the Essential Question (EQ) for this unit. The EQ is an overarching question that can relate not only to your subject area but also to the students' personal thoughts and lives. In this case the EQ is: What does it mean to "fit in?" Explain to students that they will be working to answer this question throughout the unit through many activities and experiences. Students should sit in a circle and respond to the following prompt: If you had to label yourself as one thing, what would it be?

Explore: The goal is for students to make observations about their partner. (15 minutes)

Play "Change 3 Things."

To do so, instruct students to find a partner and stand in two lines facing each other.

Give partner A one minute to observe everything about the other person's physical appearance—that is, clothing and hair.

Partner A then closes his/her eyes while partner B changes three things about his/her appearance. These changes must be visible and in clear sight.

Partner B then observes and guesses what was changed.

You can then have them try with four, five, or six changed items.

Explain: The goal is for students to understand how observations are made. (15 minutes)

Chapter Eleven

Have a discussion about what was difficult with this activity (see appendix 3).

Ask: What did you have to do to be successful in finding the changed objects?

Then ask students to take out their notebook.

Have students start by finishing the following sentence starter, "I think observation means ... ." Have students share their answers and write their answers on the board.

Create a classroom definition.

In the margins, have students answer the following question: When are some other times that you have used or heard the word observation?

Important points to teach students about observations:

- Observations are facts not opinions
- Observations use the five senses (sight, sound, taste, touch, hear)
- Observations are detailed to give clarity

In what ways are observations used in theater?

- To be able to understand how sound, lighting, and costumes affect the content of a play
- To create opinions and connections to the characters (what specific things about this play can I relate to?)
- Allows for detailed examination of characters and storylines

Elaborate: The goal is for students to continue practicing their observation skills. (15 minutes)

Play the game "Charades."

To play charades, give each student a small strip of paper.

Ask them to write a TV/movie character, a food, a sport, or an emotion on the strip.

Take the strips of paper and put them in a bowl.

Students will take turns choosing a strip of paper and performing what is on the paper.

They must do this silently with no words, using only actions.

You can choose whether or not to give students a time limit for each turn.

While playing, students in the audience should use their observational skills to conclude what the scene is about—that is, their frown means they are sad.

Students will then need to raise their hands if they think they know what is being acted out.

Tara's Tip: Some students may be out of their comfort zone with this activity. If you sense this, you can (a) help choose a paper for them that is less difficult or (b) have you or another student do the activity with them. This often helps to create trust with the student, which will aid in the community-building process.

Evaluate: The goal is for students to reflect on the observation activity. (3 minutes)

Think/pair/share: What did they have to specifically focus on to understand what was happening in each charade scene? Were any of the scenes more difficult to solve and if so, why?

The hope is for the students to connect the idea that details and close observation of those details will better allow them to understand and relate to the experiences they will have in theater.

Note: Now is the time to find a performance space for your upcoming performance. A large classroom will work fine or a cafeteria or gym. You will also want to send home an invite to parents at least two weeks prior to your performance. Make sure to include time, date, location, and a short description of what they will see.

LESSON 2: OBSERVATIONS: LEARNING TO BE MORE OBSERVANT

Student learning goals: Students will observe connections in the classroom community.

Engage: The goal is for students to make observations in the classroom. (10 minutes)

Have students observe you doing a specific task. Example: peeling an orange.

They must make at least ten written observations about you and what you are doing.

Remind students to look at their notes to ensure their observations follow the definition.

After you are finished, ask students to share their observations and discuss what made specific observations strong or weak. A strong observation includes details about what they are seeing that is a fact and not an opinion.

Strong example: You are peeling the orange in one long strip starting at the top of the orange and working your way around the orange to the bottom.

Weak example: You are peeling the orange.

Explore: The goal is for students to observe connections within the classroom. (15 minutes)

Students will pair off and go to different areas of the classroom to sit.

They will be given 5 minutes each to share an experience from their past where they were either new or felt like an outsider.

They will also have 2 minutes each to ask questions about one another's story.

Explain: The goal is for students to understand why connections are important in the classroom. (8 minutes)

Ask students to return to their seats and discuss as a class the sharing activity above.

Questions you may ask: What is something you learned about your partner? Was there something you learned about your partner that you did not know before? Did your partner reveal something about himself/herself that you can relate to or have experienced? What do you think you have gained from hearing your partner's story?

You should explain to students that learning more about their classmates is a way to observe how their worlds connect to each other.

Elaborate: The goal is for students to observe connections with classmates. (15 minutes)

Play "Cross the Line" (see appendix 4).

Students will stand in a line that is marked with tape on the floor.

Begin reading various statements; if the statement applies to the student, he or she may step over the line.

Reassure students that if they don't feel comfortable crossing the line, that it is ok and they do not have to.

Examples of possible statements can be found in appendix 4, but you may use your own discretion.

Whichever you choose, they should be thought provoking and allow for deeper exploration of self.

After each question, allow students to look around to see whom they connect with on each answer.

Evaluate: The goal is for students to reflect on today's lesson. (5 minutes)

Ticket-out-the-door: Ask each student what impressed him/her about the "Cross the Line" activity today. Did he or she learn something unexpected about another student?

LESSON 3: OBSERVATIONS: GUIDED THEATER

Student learning goals: Students will observe life experiences through guided theater.

Engage: The goal is to have students share prior knowledge of today's topic. (5 minutes)

This lesson will take place with all of the chairs and tables pushed to the walls and out of the way, leaving plenty of space for students to walk around.

Ask if anyone knows what the word "Homophobia" means?

Ask if they know what ways homophobia can be seen in schools here in the United States?

Allow some time for answers and write them on the board as the students give their examples.

Explore: The goal is for students to observe the space where the activity will occur. (8 minutes)

Have students sit anywhere they want in the room that is calm and relaxing for them, away from friends and distractions.

Have everyone close their eyes and imagine they are in a high school in the United States.

Ask questions about the space: what it looks like, smells like, what they hear, where people are in the hallways, are there adults around, what color do they imagine the hallways to be, can they hear the band playing from a classroom, does the ground feel hard, is it cold or warm in the hallway, is the hallway crammed with people or is there room to move freely, what is on the walls, what things are students or teachers talking about as they walk by, do they have friends with them, do they feel safe, and so on.

Then have them imagine they are a kid in their own school, but someone different than themselves.

Next, have them open their eyes.

Tell them that they are now in a hallway.

Ask them what they are doing in the hallway?

Tell them that when they hear the bell ring they can begin to move around the space, but they must pay close attention to everyone and everything around them. This allows for observation skills to be brought into the activity.

Play bell noise and turn on projector to show an image of a locker with the word "gay" written across it.

As students move around, bring attention to the "locker" pretending to be a fellow student who sees it.

For example: Walk up to a group of students, and say, "Oh, my gosh! Do you see what's written on that locker?"

Let students walk around and discuss this in character for a few more minutes.

Explain: The goal is for students to start discussing what is happening in this scene.

(10 minutes)

Have students freeze and come out of their character.

As a class, discuss who their character was and reflect on what they were doing.

Instruct students to write a word, sentence, or statement in response to the following (written on big paper posted around the room):

- Profile 1: Statements teachers are making about this student
- Profile 2: Statements friends and peers are making about this student
- Profile 3: Statements parents or family members are making about this student

Elaborate: The goal is for students to apply their knowledge to create a new scene.
(20 minutes)
Have students divide up into three groups.
Each group will be given either Profile 1, 2, or 3 from the big paper posted in the previous activity that they will need to create a scene with.
It must include one or more of the statements that was written by their classmates on the big paper in the previous activity. The scene must be 2–3 minutes in length, begin in tableaux, and end in one as well (here you can define tableaux). There does not need to be a clear beginning/middle/end of the scene, but can feel more like one is randomly walking in on the occurring scene.
Students will then perform the scenes for each other.
Next, have students sit in a circle and pretend there is a victim of bullying sitting in the middle.
Ask the students to say something that will encourage the student to feel better.
Students can take turns randomly stating their thoughts.
Evaluate: The goal is for students to reflect on today's activity. (10 minutes)
Reflect as a group on which statements could actually create real change in that person's life and which might cause further problems?
Ask for emotions or adjectives on how the students felt during this activity.
Ask if their feelings on bullying has changed and if they were able to relate to the person being bullied.
Discuss bullying on a local level—is it a problem at their school? How can it be changed?
For example:

1. Creating a classroom where everyone is comfortable and feels safe.
2. Creating a classroom where students can all contribute.
3. Incorporating the experiences of students into daily conversations.
4. Circle of Power and Respect (CPR; see appendix 5): Students sit in a circle at the beginning of class and there they share any shout-outs, brags,

or reminders about school or their personal life with the class. During this time, you can also play games that help reveal things about each other (i.e., Cold Wind Blows, name games).
5. Extracurricular activities offered for students to connect with other students with similar interests.
6. Do not enforce public shaming of bullies: Studies show this leads to increased bullying for students who do not like school.
7. Do not enforce zero-tolerance rules: Studies have shown that this is not effective in school systems.
8. Try and make kindness go viral in your school and community! Post positive shout-outs to students in the morning announcements or on the school website.

Finally, discuss how today's activity related to our EQ: What does it mean to "fit in?" Many times bullying is a result of someone thinking someone else does not "fit in" the way they should in the school, team, friendship group, community, or country.

Note: This lesson is modified from Jennifer Chapman's work at the University of Wisconsin–Eau Claire.

LESSON 4: CURIOSITY: I WONDER STATEMENTS

Student learning goals: Students will create "I wonder" statements about the idea of fitting in.

Engage: The goal is to engage students' curiosity skills. (5 minutes)
Show a video of a curious animal.
Example video: https://www.youtube.com/watch?v=RiVnZM1-BCY)
Ask students if the curiosity of the animal helped or hindered them in the long run? In what ways did the animal's curiosity make the students curious? Why is it important to be curious?

Explore: The goal is for students to become curious about theater and the essential question. (20 minutes)
Write the word "Theater" on the board.
Have students individually create twenty to thirty "I wonder …" statements about theater in their notebook. These statements must connect to the observations they have already made.
Allow 15 minutes for this part of the explore activity.
Have ten to fifteen students each share one of their statements.

Explain: The goal is to explain to students why curiosity is an important part to learning.
(5 minutes)

Students should learn that curiosity and brainstorming are two key parts to the learning process.

Brainstorming Rules: (a) quantity, (b) no criticism, (c) the wilder the better, and (d) hitchhiking is okay.

Brainstorming is a creativity skill that deals with new perspectives, new combinations, and new ways of thinking and doing things. The more one brainstorms, the more curious one is, which results in wanting to be engaged and learn more about a topic. "I wonder …" statements specifically allow for students to find ways they are personally connected or looking to be connected to the content.

Elaborate: The goal is for students to now brainstorm the essential question. (20 minutes)

Write the term "Fitting in" on the board.

Have students get into groups of three.

Ask students as a group to brainstorm forty to fifty "I wonder …" statements about this term.

Allow 15 minutes for this part of the elaborate activity.

Ask each group to write three of the "I wonder …" statements about fitting in on the board when they are finished.

Discuss the statements that students came up with and discuss the importance of creating these statements.

Example student statement: I wonder how theater relates to real life?

Discussion: Theater is an artistic expression of an experience; therefore, theater is simply expressing what we already see, feel, hear, touch, smell, and think about in real life. To paraphrase Oscar Wilde, theater is a way for a human being to share with another what it is to be a human being.

Take video games, for example. How many of you students play video games? And what is the main goal of your video game? (Call on someone here. Often times their video games will be about something they have never themselves experienced before: playing in the NBA, going to war, fighting aliens, etc.)

Now although you may have never experienced what is happening in your video game, you are playing a character that experiences those situations. That is what theater is: experiencing something that you may never have experienced otherwise, in a safe way. Even if you never go to war yourself, you may still experience the same emotions that a soldier does: loss, grief, mental strength, persistence, loneliness, pride, love, and so on. You can then relate to the experience of the soldier through those common feelings.

Evaluate: The goal is for students to verbalize an "I wonder …" statement to a classmate.

(3 minutes)

Think/pair/share: Have the students share one "I wonder ..." statement with another student in the room that they do not know.

LESSON 5: PROBLEM STATEMENTS

Student learning goals: Students will write problem statements.

Engage: The goal is to focus student attention on a problem. (5 minutes)

Tell students that you are really frustrated and worried—you need their help to figure out why (the scenario can be fictitious).

Have students ask you questions to help clarify why you are frustrated and worried.

If students don't know where to start have them ask questions regarding who, what, why, and where.

Have students help you figure out the reason why you are frustrated/worried and explain.

Explore: The goal is for students to experience how problems develop. (5 minutes)

Give students one of the following observations:

1. I am mad at my best friend.
2. This pen is blue.
3. My best friend is not talking to me.

Have them list five answers to why the observation exists (Why am I mad at my best friend?)

Have them choose one of their five answers.

Next have them ask why again to that answer five times (it is ok if the responses either narrow or broaden the question).

Explain: The goal is for students to be able to understand how problems develop. (10 minutes)

Discuss how all problems are based on observations (refer to engage activity).

A problem is half solved if it is properly stated (refer to engage activity).

Tara's Tip: This is a great place to address real problems the students face in their lives. Many times students are upset and frustrated and angry and don't know exactly why. By identifying the specific problem, it can help them understand and overcome many of these emotions.

Discuss how many different problems can exist for the same situation (refer to Explore activity).

Elaborate: The goal is for students to be able to write a problem statement. (25 minutes)

Have them list twenty-five "I Wonder …" statements using their best observations that begin with the following words: "I wonder …

Tara's Tip: Students will really struggle with this. They will want to know what the right answer is. It is important to stress that there is no right answer right now. Encourage them to think about what they want to know about the activity—emphasize curiosity!

Have students change each "I Wonder …" statement into a problem statement by doing the following:

Determining	Calculating
Solving	Convincing
Understanding	Finding
Communicating	Explaining
Defining	

Change the words "I wonder" to "The problem is …"

Follow this phrase with a cue word such as the following:

It is important to discuss at this point that the problem statements are action orientated.

Students should have twenty-five problem statements developed from their "I wonder …" statements.

Evaluate: The goal is for students to be able to critique and identify correctly written problem statements. (20 minutes)

Have students exchange problem statements with another student.

Students make edits and corrections as needed.

Students write their edited problem statements on the board (this may need to be done in two or three shifts depending on class size).

Tara's Tip: This is an important exercise in helping students to give and receive feedback. Students will be learning a more detailed way of giving feedback in Lesson 11. I found it to be important to lay some ground rules when giving and receiving feedback, such as there are no personal criticisms, suggestions must be specific, you should provide both positive and constructive feedback, it's ok to ask clarifying questions, and so on. If this is done correctly, it can build a lot of trust between students. It is important to remember that students are not choosing a problem to design an experiment yet—this is all about writing correct problem statements—choosing a problem statement is the next lesson. Students may edit and change problem statements as needed as they receive feedback from the class.

LESSON 6: GATHERING INFORMATION: VOICE

Student learning goals: Students will explore how they use their voice in theater.

Engage: The goal is for students to observe the way they can use their voice in theater. (5 minutes)

Show students a clip of a human beat box machine: https://www.youtube.com/watch?v=TQFTAXTGHm0.

Ask students what part of their mouth did the beatboxer use?

Show students a clip of a person creating multiple accents: https://www.youtube.com/watch?v=3UgpfSp2t6k.

Have students hypothesize how the actors in the clip achieved these sounds.

Tara's Tip: If any student can beat box or create accents/voices this would be a good time to allow him/her to display those skills.

Explore: The goal is for students to explore their ability to use their voice. (15 minutes)

Play the game "Soundscapes."

To do this students sit in a circle while one student leaves the room entirely.

The circle should then brainstorm a place that is well known and they could recreate using bodily sounds (beach, mall, football game, zoo, busy street, etc.).

The circle must create sounds that they connect to the given location.

Once the students are clear on what sound they will be making, have the student return to class, and stand in the middle of the circle with closed eyes.

Instruct the circle to begin creating their soundscape.

Then give the person in the middle a chance to guess what the location is.

Tara's Tip: Before beginning, discuss with students what the term soundscape means. Start by discussing what a landscape is and see if a student can define it (visible features of an area or land). Then ask students if they can then infer what a soundscape is based off of their definition of landscape. A soundscape is the sounds that are associated with a certain area or land. Then assign students in the circle to possible different location sounds before beginning the soundscape so it stays focused. Also remind students about the noise levels in the given locations; that is, the beach isn't just loud seagulls squawking.

Explain: The goal is for students to learn about how they use their voice in theater. (20 minutes)

Define "voice" as: oral sounds used to project words and create character.

Have students guess what their articulators are.

Define "articulators" as: the parts of the mouth they use to pronounce words (lips, teeth, tip of tongue).

Define "resonators" as: the parts of the body that help to create their vocal sound (chest, top of head, mouth, nasal).

Discuss how variations of how articulators and resonators are used can create many different sounds in the way words are projected to create character on stage.

Define what it means to project your voice: speaking loudly and clearly for the audience to hear.

Elaborate: The goal is for students to apply their knowledge of their voices in multiple vocal exercises. (10 minutes)

Have students try a number of tongue twisters that are displayed on the board to practice the use of their articulators.

Examples:

"The lips, the teeth, the tip of the tongue. The tip of the tongue, the teeth, the lips."

Repeat the phrase "Toy Boat" five times fast.

"Sally sells seashells by the seashore."

"Can a can can a can as a canner can can a can?"

Go through various vocal exercises with students to show them how to warm up their voice.

Examples:

Lip and tongue trills

Stretching and massaging their mouths and cheeks

"Woo" whistles from high to low and from low to high

Discuss the different parts of the mouth they use for each of these. Example: "Woo" whistles require your lips to make an "O" shape and your tongue to lay flat in your mouth.

Tara's Tip: One way to get students thinking about how we use our articulators is to challenge them to say the alphabet without moving any parts of their mouth. Students will assume that this is something they can easily do. Ask for a few volunteers to try it in front of the class—they will quickly realize it is impossible. For any sound to be made other than "eh," you must be able to move a part of your mouth. This challenge helps students to better understand why articulation is so important in forming clear words on stage.

Evaluate: The goal is to evaluate what students have learned about an actor's voice.

As each student exits, they must create a sound with their voice and then tell you what articulator and/or resonator they used. (3 minutes)

LESSON 7: GATHERING INFORMATION: SPACE

Student learning goals: Students will demonstrate their learned knowledge of the theater space and how to use it.

Engage: The goal is for students to engage in a performance that involves extensive blocking. (5 minutes)

Show students a Cirque de Soleil performance: https://vimeo.com/37606291.

Ask students about the movement on stage: What do they think the practice regimen was like?

What did the actors have to think about prior to the show for the performance to be successful?

Explore: The goal is for students to explore movement on stage. (15 minutes)

Have students get into groups of three.

Give each student in the group a prewritten script (see appendix 6).

Ask students to individually come up with at least three different movements to write into their script at any spot they choose. The movements must involve crossing the stage in any direction they choose.

Ask each group to come on stage and read their lines while performing their movements. This will most likely end with students running into each other and the lines not being congruent with the actions.

Explain: The goal is for students to learn that stage blocking is intentional. (15 minutes)

Ask students what was difficult about the activity and what would have made it easier?

Define "stage blocking" as: the exact movement of an actor on stage.

Discuss why stage blocking is important: Actors know where they will be moving at every point of the scene.

Discuss who blocks a scene: Playwright, director, choreographer, or actor.

Talk about general blocking: exit, enter, crossing.

Relate the importance of meaningful blocking; that is, don't have them move unless it absolutely makes sense with the content of the line/scene. Whatever movement is done must be representative of a real-life similar situation and must be believable to your audience.

Discuss the importance of the actor's body and face being seen for the majority of the lines. Why? Facial expressions, gestures, body language.

Define "stage directions" as: the mapping-out of the stage space.

Define the various stage directions and create a map showing them where these spaces exist (see appendix 6).

Elaborate: The goal is for students to practice moving to the different stage directions using specific blocking. (15 minutes)

Have students get back into their groups of three.

Assign one person as the director and two people as the actors.

Give students a blocking sheet with five blank spaces for blocking (see appendix 8).

Ask the directors to decide on three of the movements and ask the actors to agree on the remaining two.

Remind students that their movements must be meaningful and make sense with the script.

Have students perform their scenes for the group.

Discuss the successes of the scenes.

Evaluate: The goal is to evaluate the students' knowledge of the stage space. (3 minutes)

As each student leaves, they must first run to a stage direction that you shout out.

They must go to the back of the line if they did not get it right the first time.

LESSON 8: GATHERING INFORMATION: WRITING SCRIPTS

Student learning goals: Students will practice writing scripts.

Engage: The goal is to engage students in the process of script writing by exposing them to work of famous playwrights or scriptwriters. (8 minutes)

Show students a clip from an interview with a scriptwriter: https://www.youtube.com/watch?v=TPHHelpkpEY. (Stop at 4 minutes)

Discuss the video and what they learned.

Explore: The goal is for students to observe the differences and similarities between a script and a novel. (15 minutes)

At their table have students look at a script from a popular play like "Our Town."

Ask them to go through and make ten observations about the script.

Ask students to them take out a novel of their own or from your library/in-class book collection and make ten observations about the novel.

They must then make a separate compare-and-contrast list of differences between a novel and a script.

Your goal is for them to point out that a script lists its action and lines differently from a novel. They might also observe that both books and scripts have titles and chapters, but chapters are listed as scenes in the script. They might also point out the difference in spacing of a script versus a novel.

Discuss the observations as a class and make a list on the board.

Explain: The goal is for students to learn how to write a script. (7 minutes)

Describe to students how a script is set up and show them the two major ways of writing a script (see appendix 9).

Elaborate: The goal is for students to practice writing a script for a scene from a popular fairytale. (15 minutes)

Randomly assign students a scene from a popular fairytale or children's story. For example: Cinderella's time at the ball, Snow White meeting the seven dwarves, Mufasa and the stampede in *The Lion King*, Ariel first walking on land, Hansel and Gretel meeting the evil witch.

Give each student a brief summary of the scene so they know what happens and which characters should be involved.

Students must then write a script for the scene.

Evaluate: The goal is for students to demonstrate their ability to write a script. (8 minutes)

Request students to turn in their scripts.

Randomly pick a script and call up the number of students needed to perform the scene.

Ask the students to perform the scene.

Discuss the successes and possible failures of the scene based on the writing. Do not call out names of students who wrote the scenes, but make sure to discuss the failures as edits to future editions of the scene. Remind students that failure is an important part of writing scripts and should be expected (we will cover the specifics of feedback in Lesson 11). The focus should be on what was successful from their draft and what they can improve on for their future draft.

Repeat with a new script as time allows.

LESSON 9: GATHERING INFORMATION: COSTUMES

Student learning goals: Students will analyze costumes and their importance in a performance.

Engage: The goal is to foster student curiosity in costuming. (5 minutes)

Watch a behind-the-scenes video from a Broadway musical that discusses how costumes are designed for a performance.

Explore: The goal is for students to recognize that clothing has an effect on the portrayal of a character. (10 minutes)

Have students pair up.

Each group will then have the chance to go into the costume closet. Items that might be in your costume closet are: hats, coats, capes, dresses, uniforms, scarves, or ties. While there, they must choose two articles of clothing for their partner to wear over their own clothes.

After everyone has chosen their items have them stand in a circle so that they can observe what each other is wearing.

Ask students to look around and choose one person. With that person in mind, they need to decide what kind of personality the character would be in a play. Would they play the villain, the hero, the princess/prince, the cranky old man/woman, or the jokester?

Ask students to defend their answers based on what the two articles of clothing are that the other person is wearing.

Explain: The goal is for students to understand the purpose of costume design. (10 minutes)

Define "costume design" as: creating and putting together clothing used in a performance.

Discuss the purpose of costumes and their specific designs: It creates the personality of the character and helps tell the story of the play.

Talk about the history of costuming: First forms were masks, men portraying female roles, and official costume designing began in the 1700s.

Discuss what to keep in mind when designing a costume:

- The vision:
  - Setting of scene including time, place, and culture
  - Action in costume
  - Color scheme
  - Materials available (rent, borrow, buy)

Elaborate: The goal is for students to try to design a costume for a character from a story using the above criteria. (25 minutes)

Read a short story.

While reading create a list of main characters on the board.

When finished, have students help you create a thought map of the setting and vision for a possible production of this story.

Have students also decide on general facts about each character (age, gender, personality).

Each student will then be given a template of a human to create a costume design on. Students should start by creating a vision statement for the character they choose and then design the costume according to that vision.

Tara's Tip: Choose a story that most students are unfamiliar with like "High and Lifted Up" by Mike Krath, "The Lottery" by Shirley Jackson, "The Gift of the Magi" by O. Henry, or even a story you make up yourself. This will allow for them to use their imagination instead of prior knowledge of the characters to create their design.

Evaluate: The goal is for students to demonstrate their knowledge of costume design.

(3 minutes)

Students will show their final designs to the class and submit them.

LESSON 10: GATHERING INFORMATION: SET DESIGN

Student learning goals: Students will study set designs and create a small set design for a production.

Engage: The goal is to engage students in the process of designing a set. (5 minutes)

Watch a behind-the-scenes look at the designing and creating of a set design (*Shrek The Musical* set design: https://www.youtube.com/watch?v=68Mig6ni0vU).

Discuss what the designer said about what went into the designing of a set and what criteria they had to keep in mind when designing the set.

Explain: The goal is to explain to students what set design is and discuss the criteria for a successful set design. (10 minutes)

Define "set design" as: the planning and creating of the environment of a play.

Explain to the students how the set helps to tell the story of the play.

A set includes, but is not limited to: backdrops, platforms, furniture, and anything that hangs from the rails.

Special criteria to consider when designing a set:

- The vision of the production:
  - Setting of scene including time, place, and culture
  - Color scheme
- Any distinct needs such as a tower, beanstalk, house that you can see into, and so on.
- Materials available: No matter what your budget is, your job is to be creative with the materials you have—the audience needs to believe that the set is realistic and believable in order to transport the audience to the setting of the play.

Define and show examples of a rendering (see appendix 10): a drawing of a proposed set.

Define and show examples of a scale model: a smaller 3D representation of the set.

Define what a prop is: a handheld object used by an actor on stage.

Discuss the use of props in a show and why they are helpful in telling the story of the play.

Elaborate: The goal is for students to create a rendering of a set design based on a well-known fairytale. (30 minutes)

Each group will create a vision statement for their final design.

Students will need to work with a partner to create a rendering for a set from a well-known fairytale.

For example:

- Cinderella
- Little Red Riding Hood
- Hansel and Gretel

- Goldilocks
- Snow White
- Three Little Pigs

They must follow the criteria listed above, but can imagine that their budget for materials is limitless.

Evaluate: The goal is for students to present their knowledge of set design through a final rendering of a set. (8 minutes)

Each student will come in front of the class to read his or her vision statement and display their completed rendering.

Students will then submit the rendering for a grade.

LESSON 11: GATHERING INFORMATION: FEEDBACK AND FEEDFORWARD

Student learning goals: Students will learn about feedback as they continue planning their performances.

Engage: The goal is for students to observe a performance from a Broadway musical.

(10 minutes)

Show students a scene from the Broadway musical *Hamilton*: http://www.slate.com/blogs/browbeat/2016/02/15/watch_the_cast_of_hamilton_perform_the_musical_s_electrifying_opening_number.html.

Explore: The goal is for students to begin to understand what makes a successful performance for this project. (10 minutes)

Prompt students through a discussion about the performance. What went well? What could they (the actors) do better for the next rehearsal or performance?

Explain: The goal is for students to understand what positive and constructive feedback can do to help create a successful final performance. (15 minutes)

Begin by reviewing criteria that an expert may look at when determining if a performance is successful:

- Projection of voice
- Articulation of lines
- Clear and intentional movement
- Facial expressions matching the mood of the character
- An engaging performance

Explain to students the difference between positive and constructive performance.

Positive: What went well/what should NOT be changed
Constructive: What needs work/suggestions for improvement

Tara's Tip: It does not help a performer to simply know what didn't go well with a performance. They then need guidance as to how to improve the performance. Use the following equation when giving feedback in the classroom:

Positive + Positive + Positive + Problem + Solution = Successful Feedback

The main point is to always have more positive feedback than constructive and always end with concrete ways they can improve. A 3:1 ratio is considered the best ratio for positive to constructive feedback.

You must also be sure that you are being specific!

Example of successful feedback equation: "Great annunciation during the bullying scene. Nice job at facing out toward your audience. One thing you could work on is your projection. Here's a way that you can work on this: stand on one side of your backyard and read your lines to a friend or family member who are standing across the yard from you. Ask them to give you feedback on your projection."

Discuss with students why "That was good" or "That was bad" are poor examples of feedback.

Elaborate: The goal is for students to practice giving feedback. (10 minutes)

Watch a short video of a talent/performance competition on YouTube and note the feedback from the judges on the show. Pick one that demonstrates good feedback. Example clip: http://www.youtube.com/watch?v=v0JPKioIHiM.

Ask students to pick out the positive and constructive feedback that the judges gave.

Have them define what made it good feedback.

Watch a second short video of a performance and demonstrate feedback for your students. Example clip: https://www.youtube.com/watch?v=xlbDHejQFV4.

Evaluate: The goal is for students to demonstrate their knowledge of successful feedback. (8 minutes)

Students must fill out a "Ticket out the door" that gives five pieces of feedback for a short performance video.

Prior to the start of the video, review the parts to successful feedback and remind students to be specific. Example clip from the Katy Perry Superbowl halftime show: https://www.youtube.com/watch?v=-1cyCmUdDNQ.

LESSON 12: CREATE: PICK AND PLAN

Student learning goals: Students will create written pieces inspired from their own experiences.

Engage: The goal is for students to continue to explore what "fitting in" means. (5 minutes)

Share the essential question with the class: What does it mean to "fit in?" Write the term "fitting in" on the whiteboard.

Ask students to come up with three sentences where they can use this term.

Have students share their responses and discuss the different ways the term was used.

Specifically discuss anyone who used the term as a way of being accepted by others.

Explore: The goal is to help students connect the EQ to their personal experiences. (15 minutes)

Think/pair/share:

Think: Ask students to respond to the following journal prompt: When was a time that you struggled with fitting in?

Tell students they must write for the entire 10 minutes.

Possible things they could write about when they think they've run out of things to write: Emotions during this situation, describe the people involved, use your five senses to describe what you remember from the situation, tell the reader why this situation stuck out to you.

Pair: Pair up with a partner once the 10 minutes are up and share for 2 minutes each a summary of what you wrote.

Share: Ask for five students to share a summary of what they wrote.

Explain: The goal is for students to understand the final performance and its requirements. (15 minutes)

Tell students that they will be creating a performance piece based on a select number of journal responses that were just created. Let them know about those written pieces that you will be choosing, to be performed, once they are submitted. Students can opt out if they don't feel comfortable sharing their story in public.

Tell students that they will be working in groups of three. Everyone will be a primary in their own performance, but they can also choose to be a secondary actor in a different group if needed.

Explain to students they will be in charge of costume selection, set design, and script writing for the entirety of the scene. Each person in the group will have a job that they will be in charge of fulfilling.

Discuss the scoring guide for the final performance (see appendix 11).

Elaborate: The goal is to share responses to the prompt to begin the selection process of the stories. (15 minutes)

Students who are open to their stories being shared will then read their responses aloud to the group.

Evaluate: The goal is to select the stories that will be performed. (3 minutes)

Have those students turn in their responses for you to select from.

Tara's Tip: If not enough students are willing to share their events, have all students turn in their work and then ask specific writers if they would allow their stories to be chosen and performed anonymously. With the final group of stories, create groups based on the needs for the story (character list will play a role in group choices). You can also think about putting groups together based on how well you believe they will work together. Often it is good to mix students up depending on how assertive a student is. Grouping all assertive students together might result in a power struggle, while putting all passive students together may result in a lack of effort or direction.

LESSON 13: CREATE: COMPOSE

Student learning goals: Students will begin composing their performances.

Engage: The goal is for students to observe a performance from last year. (10 minutes)

Show students a recording from last year's performances.

Explore: The goal is for students to share their stories with their groups. (10 minutes)

Assign groups for the performances and ask students whose stories were chosen at the end of last class to share them with their group.

If any students in the group have questions about the stories, remind them to ask clarifying questions.

Below is a list of questions that a student may have for the writer:

How would you describe the personality of this character?

What is the setting for this story?

What mood is the character in for this scene?

How does this character carry himself/herself or speak?

Explain: The goal is for students to learn what makes a story's structure successful to a viewer. (10 minutes)

Explain to students what a story arc is (see appendix 12).

Most stories naturally flow through this arc making it easier for the viewer/reader to understand the plot of the story. Their stories will require them to follow the natural progression of a story arc.

Reassure students that if their current stories don't fit into a story arc perfectly, they will have the opportunity to alter their stories slightly.

Elaborate: The goal is for students to create a story arc for their story. (20 minutes)

Assign groups the task of filling out a story arc for their scene (see appendix 12).

Have groups assign a scribe, timekeeper, question master, volume controller, and task manager. The scribe will be in charge of filling out the story arc for the assigned story. The timekeeper will manage the clock and remind the group when they must move on due to time constraints. The question master will be in charge of asking the teacher questions if the group has any. The volume controller will be in charge of reminding their group-mates of suggested volume levels when working in small groups. The task manager will make sure all voices are heard and no one is being excluded from the assignment.

Meet with each group briefly to ensure they understand the assignment and will be ready for tomorrow's work.

Evaluate: The goal is for students to reflect on their connection to their group's story. (3 minutes)

Ticket-out-the-door: What is one way you can connect to the story that you will be performing? How do you see the issue of fitting in occur in this story?

LESSON 14: CREATE: COMPOSE

Student learning goals: Students will continue to plan and create their performances.

Engage: The goal is for students to learn the importance of following structure with their performances. (8 minutes)

Ask students to sit in a circle.

As a group they will create a story. Each person is allowed to add one word to the story. Start with one person in the group and go around the circle until everyone has added a word.

Keep track of the story on paper or with a recording device and share the story once it has ended with the last person in the circle.

Discuss how the lack of structure to this story made it come out sounding silly.

Often, there will be no clear ending to the story.

Discuss what this as an audience member makes you think/feel about the story.

Explore: The goal is for students to create a script from their story arc/story. (20 minutes)

Briefly review the script-writing format (see appendix 13).

Students should begin writing their script.

Tara's Tip: You can have students stay in their roles from yesterday's group time or have them switch it up depending on how it went.

Explain: The goal is for students to conference with you to gain feedback on their script. (5 minutes)

Throughout the writing process, conference with each group to ensure they are on the right track with their script. Checking in with each group every 10–12 minutes will help ensure that they are on a successful path.

Give any necessary feedback.

Elaborate: The goal is for students to apply verbal feedback from you. (17 minutes)

Students should continue to work on their script making edits that were suggested.

Evaluate: The goal is for students to turn in their scripts for feedback. (3 minutes)

Have students turn in scripts for final written feedback from you.

Tara's Tip: Make copies of the script for the next class period so each student in the group has his or her own script. You can also assign each group a folder that you keep at the end of class. The folder can be used to keep their scripts and any other assignments for the performance during this unit.

LESSON 15: CREATE: REVIEW AND REVISE

Student learning goals: Students will finish their scripts and begin blocking/rehearsing their scenes.

Engage: The goal is for students to warm-up for rehearsal today. (5 minutes)

Run through a quick voice and body warm-up.

You can use a vocal warm-up from Lesson 6.

Body warm-up examples:

Roll shoulders up and around

Roll neck around both ways

Shake out each limb for 10 seconds

Stretch and massage the mouth and cheeks

Explore: The goal is for students to finish their scripts. (10 minutes)

Students should continue revising their scripts using the feedback they received.

Explore: The goal is for students to begin blocking their scenes. (10 minutes)

Students should begin blocking their scenes in an assigned space.

Explain: The goal is for students to review the scoring guide. (5 minutes)

Review the scoring guide and answer any questions (see appendix 11).

Elaborate: The goal is for students to begin applying the scoring guide to their performances. (20 minutes)

Students should continue blocking their performances while using the scoring guide as a checklist.

Example checklist for today:

1. Focus on creating clear and intentional movement where your audience can always see your face when you have a line.
2. Once you believe you have achieved this checkpoint above, see your teacher for feedback.
3. Continue rehearsing using the feedback from your teacher.

Evaluate: The goal is for students to self-evaluate their progress thus far. (3 minutes)

Have groups grade themselves with the scoring guide based on the current status of their performances.

Tara's Tip: For students who are performing in multiple scenes, help them create a rehearsal schedule each day that allows them time to work with each of the groups as needed.

LESSON 16: CREATE: REVIEW

Student learning goals: Students will perform their scenes for feedback.

Engage: The goal is for students to warm-up for rehearsal today. (5 minutes)

Run through a quick voice and body warm-up.

See Lessons 6 and 15 for ideas.

Explore: The goal is for students to continue rehearsing their scenes. (15 minutes)

Allow for rehearsal time. Continue to either display or give students copies of the performance criteria.

Give students a checklist for what they must accomplish daily. Today's checklist would look like this:

1. Review criteria as a group.
2. Focus on projection and articulation of lines.
3. If you finish within the 15 minutes, practice your lines for your group members and have them give you feedback.

Explain: The goal is for students to understand how they will be giving/receiving feedback today. (5 minutes)

Explain to students that they will be performing their scenes for each other today.

While they are performing, videotape each group for further self-reflection during next class.

They will not be critiqued on their set or costumes.

Each group will be required to give verbal feedback to one other group using the feedback guidelines. The scoring guide should be available for students to give feedback with.

Elaborate: The goal is for students to perform for verbal feedback. (25 minutes)

The class will form an audience.

Each group should perform for written/verbal feedback from one other group (see appendix 14). (You can also add in feedback or help clarify feedback if needed.)

The feedback can be given at the end of each performance or at the end of class.

For the group giving the feedback, the scribe should write down the feedback onto the Feedback Form (see appendix 14) for the performing group to reflect on during the next class.

Evaluate: The goal is for students to give feedback in a meaningful way. (3 minutes)

Have the scribes turn in the feedback and check that their critique follows the requirements.

LESSON 17: CREATE: REVISE

Student learning goals: Students will apply feedback to their performance.

Engage: The goal is for students to self-critique their performances using the videos from last class. (10 minutes)

Allow for students to view their performances on individual tablets or as a class.

Each group should then write down at least five pieces of feedback for their performance.

Explore: The goal is for students to apply their feedback to their performances. (20 minutes)

Students will then discuss with their group what went well and what they can improve upon.

Students will then start to apply the feedback to their performances.

Explain: The goal is for students to conference with you to discuss feedback and application. (5 minutes)

Each group will meet with you to discuss the feedback they received and how they are going to apply it to their own work (see appendix 14).

Tara's Tip: Students will tend to take the feedback far more negatively than intended. Help guide the students through application of their feedback and continue to encourage them to show how the feedback is helping them. It's important to discuss with students that perfection does not come in a day or two and that if they are not instantly successful that does not mean they are terrible thespians. You can connect this to sports, musical talents, and even teaching!

Elaborate: The goal is for students to continue rehearsing using the feedback provided.

(15 minutes)

Once you have met with the groups individually, instruct them to continue rehearsing specifically focusing on the feedback provided.

Evaluate: The goal is for students to evaluate their progress with their scenes thus far.

(3 minutes)

Ask each group to fill out a scoring guide for their performance based on their current progress.

Ask students to turn in the scoring guides (see appendix 11).

LESSON 18: CREATE: CONSTRUCT

Student learning goals: Students will plan and create the setting and costumes for their scenes.

Engage: The goal is for students to reflect on the feedback they have been receiving. (5 minutes)

Large group prompt: What was a piece of feedback they received yesterday that was especially helpful in their group's progress?

Have each group come up with one answer and share with class.

Explore: The goal is for students to begin exploring what their set and costumes will look like. (10 minutes)

Give each group three Costume Worksheets (see appendix 15).

At the top of the worksheets have students label their character in the scene.

Ask students to use the worksheet to create a drawing or list of characteristics for what they envision their character wearing.

Give each group one Set Design Worksheet (see appendix 16).

Ask each group to create a rendering or list characteristics of what they believe the set should look like using their blocking as a guide.

Explain: The goal is for students to review the requirements for creating sets and costumes. (10 minutes)

Review with students what goes into planning costumes for their classroom performances.

- The vision:
    - Setting of scene including time, place, and culture
    - Action in costume

- Color scheme
- Materials available (rent, borrow, buy)

Review with students what goes into planning set designs for their classroom performances.

- The vision of the production:
  - Setting of scene including time, place, and culture
  - Color scheme
- Any distinct needs such as a tower, beanstalk, house that you can see into, and so on.
- Materials available: No matter what your budget is, your job is to be creative with the materials you have—the audience needs to believe that the set is realistic and believable in order to transport the audience to the setting of the play.

Remind students that you are not expecting their costumes and set to be that of a professional performance but that thoughtful planning is still required for both.

Tara's Tip: If you have access to a costume/set/prop closet, utilize this as much as possible for these performances to cut down on extra work and/or expenses.

Elaborate: The goal is for students to begin planning their set and costumes for their scene. (25 minutes)

Give students a Set and Costume Planning Worksheet (see appendix 17).

Instruct students how to fill out the worksheet. Ask them to use full sentences when describing their visions. Instruct students to include character names for any costumes that are needed.

Evaluate: The goal is for students to gain approval for costume and set plans. (3 minutes)

Instruct students once they've filled out the worksheets to then conference with you to approve ideas.

LESSON 19: CREATE: TEST

Student learning goals: Students will learn how to implement their plans for their set/costumes.

Engage: The goal is for students to reflect on their learning process thus far. (5 minutes)

Quick writing journal prompt: What has been your favorite part of the process so far (set, costume, script writing, acting, etc.)?

Turn in prompt.

Explore: The goal is for students to choose their costumes/set pieces/props. (15 minutes)

Introduce students to your classroom collection of costumes, set pieces, and props.

Allow students to find their costumes and any set pieces or props they might need.

Explain: The goal is to conference over costume/set pieces/props. (5 minutes)

Meet with groups to discuss their choices and question any issues you might see (see appendix 17).

Remind students that when using these items, only use what is necessary in matching their vision for their scene.

The final decision should be ultimately up to them, but they will need to be able to defend their choices if questioned for their final grade.

Elaborate: The goal is for students to rehearse using their costumes/set pieces/props. (25 minutes)

Instruct students to now rehearse with their costumes, set pieces, and props. Check in with each group throughout the rehearsal time to ensure that the set pieces, props, and costumes will work well for the scene.

Allow for any changes that need to be made to these items as they are rehearsing.

Evaluate: The goal is for students to evaluate how rehearsal went today and determine any needs for next rehearsal. (3 minutes)

Ask groups to respond to the following writing prompt:

- Write one sentence reflecting on how today's rehearsal went.
- Make a list of any costumes, props, or set pieces you need to bring from home or buy for the performance.
- What is your goal for the next class time?

Students should individually respond to the second prompt in their planner as well.

Ask students to turn in the assignment.

LESSON 20: CREATE: TEST

Student learning goals: Students will perform a dress rehearsal for the class and teacher.

Engage: The goal is for students to reflect on the upcoming performance. (5 minutes)

Ask students to sit in a circle and respond to the following prompt: What is one thing you are excited or nervous about for the final performance?

Explain: The goal is to explain the process of a dress rehearsal and scoring guide. (10 minutes)

Explain the process of a dress rehearsal. What will the show look like? What will the order be? Is there a reason for that order? What costumes, set pieces, props, sound, and lighting will be needed?

Make sure all students are clear on the expectations of being backstage and onstage, that is, no talking, breaking character, and so on.

Review the scoring guide as a group (see appendix 11).

Elaborate: The goal is for students to prepare for the dress rehearsal. (10 minutes)

Have students gather all set pieces, props, and costumes and rehearse.

Evaluate: The goal is for students to run through a dress rehearsal. (28 minutes)

Run through a full dress rehearsal.

Write down any last-minute critiques for each group as they perform to be given to them at the beginning of the next class.

LESSON 21A: PERFORM (IN-CLASS)

Engage: The goal is for students to warm up for their performance. (5 minutes)

Lead the students through a voice and body warm-up (see Lessons 6 and 15).

Explore: The goal is for students to run through their scenes. (10 minutes)

As the students run a final rehearsal, give any last pieces of critique to each group.

Explain: The goal is to give students last-minute notes/advice for the performance. (5 minutes)

Gather the students together and remind them of any last notes for etiquette during the performances.

Elaborate/Evaluate: The goal is to perform for an audience. (30 minutes)

Perform for an outside audience. This can be other classes of students, parents, teachers, community members, and so on.

Use the scoring guide to evaluate each performance.

Record the performances for future reflection.

Tara's Tip: You may also choose to use the recordings to grade the performances at another time. Find two students who can help with recording when they are not acting in a scene—this allows for students to be a part of the production process. If you choose to use light or sound effects, students can also help with these areas to further their knowledge of backstage theater work.

LESSON 21B: EVENING PERFORMANCE—SHOWCASE EVENT

In order to allow parents, community members, school board members, and faculty to be a part of this experience, you may also hold an evening performance. A large part of gaining respect for a theater department requires community members to see your program as a prestigious part of the school's curriculum.

Alternative: If student attendance at night is problematic you could have the students video-record their in-class performances and then show the recordings at night for the parents/guardians and other school staff.

LESSON 22: ANALYSIS OF THE ENTIRE INQUIRY PROCESS

Student learning goal: Students will analyze their performances and reflect on the process.

Engage: The goal is for students to begin reflecting on the videos of their performances. (30 minutes)

Watch the performances as a class.

Explore: The goal is for students to respond to prompts about the performance. (6 minutes)

Ask students to sit in a circle with their groups and respond to the following three prompts:

- What I just saw was …
- The hardest part of this was …
- The part I liked the most was …

Explain: The goal is for students to share their answers to the prompts. (5 minutes)

As a large group, discuss with students their answers to these questions.

Explain to students that this entire unit circles back to the EQ that was first asked: What does "fitting in" mean?

Elaborate: The goal is for students to complete a written reflection worksheet. (10 minutes)

Hand out the Performance Reflection Worksheet (see appendix 18).
Evaluate: The goal is for students to submit their reflections for a grade. (3 minutes)
Ask students to hand in the assignment for a grade. (12 points)

LESSON 23: CONCLUSION: WHAT HAVE WE LEARNED?

Student learning goals: Students will create conclusions on what they have learned during this unit in terms of (a) content (theater) and (b) process (creating theater as a team).

Engage: The goal is for students to answer the EQ: What does it mean to "fit in?" (5 minutes)
Sit in a circle with a ball.
One person will start with the ball and answer the following prompt from the worksheet:
Fitting in means ...
The first person will then throw the ball to a new person who will also respond to the prompt.
The ball should continue being passed until everyone has had it once.
Explain: The goal is for students to understand the purpose of this unit. (5 minutes)
Explain to students that the goal with learning is to end up having a change in their thoughts, beliefs, or actions.
Ask students to raise their hand if their thoughts, beliefs, or actions were changed from this performance and study of "fitting in."
Allow for sharing supporting these changes.
Elaborate: The goal is for students to share their thoughts with a partner. (10 minutes)
Think/pair/share the following prompts:

- What are three things you have learned about in theater that you didn't know before (i.e., set design, costume design, using your voice in theater, script writing, stage blocking)?
- What have you learned specifically about "fitting in?"
- What do you now believe about "fitting in?"
- How does this connect to your lives outside of school?

Evaluate: The goal is for students to share their thoughts with the class. (10 minutes)
Ask each student to share one answer from the prompts with the group as a whole.

Celebrate the class success by ending with a game that congratulates one another.

Tara's Tip: Play the yarn web game. One person starts with a ball of yarn and holds onto the end. They chose a second person to throw the ball to and compliment on their work this unit (this should be specific and meaningful). Each time a person gets the ball they must hold onto the yarn in front of them before throwing the ball to a new person. By the end of the game, each person will have had the ball once, received one compliment, and created a giant web showing the interconnectedness that occurred throughout this unit.

Conclusion

We (the authors) have been involved with athletics (sports) for our whole lives, as: players, assistant coaches, coaches, volunteers, and parents. Some of those experiences were just fantastic—they were fun, the people were excellent, and the seasons were viewed as "successful." They changed people's lives.

Some of those experiences were less than stellar—for any number of reasons: a personal lack of commitment, the other players, or coaches who were so concerned with winning (or a total lack thereof) that the individuals were left behind.

Those "sports" experiences are mirrored by our experiences as students and teachers. In some classes we learned a lot—about ourselves, about content, and about life itself. Some (many perhaps) mirrored the less-than-stellar type of experience: little relevance, no passion, or no connection to our lives as individuals.

Brainball (Theater Edition [TE]) attempts to blend the best of both worlds. That means the goal is clear, everyone has an important role, and that the learning itself is explicit, relevant, and public. It is intended to explicitly change people's lives, to help them grow into their potentialities and become the person they dream of becoming.

The challenge as coach (teacher) of Brainball (TE) is our own personal learning journey. Not having the played the game ourselves makes the transition into "coach" more complicated than we might prefer. When going through the learning process, we have found it helpful to focus on the stages of the Hero's Journey: (a) Innocence Lost; (b) Chaos and Complexity; (c) The Heroic Quest; (d) Guru's and Alliances; (e) Trials, Tests, and Initiations; and (f) Insight and Transformations. These are the stages of personal transformation.

Great learning is the result of learning adventures—and most adventures appear awesome in hindsight (not so much when you are in the midst of it!). Transformative learning adventures are best done with others (a team). They provide support—emotional, social, intellectual, physical, and moral support—when it is needed (not before and not when it is too late). People who are members of great teams have their individual goals met while helping the team (and others) meet the larger team goal as well—it is truly a win–win scenario.

The beauty of the game is that it is a learning journey for everyone! There is always more to learn about: yourself, others, the process, and the content. True learning means coming to understand how shallow your current learning really is—and that is okay. Journeys are not destinations—they value the process, the product, and the community with whom the journey was taken.

Finally, while it is wonderful to coach a team of highly skilled players, it is perhaps even more fulfilling to take an average team and coach them into greatness. In Brainball (TE) that means coaching people to live the process of science in their daily lives, to work effectively with others to accomplish something important, and to use content to answer important questions or solve real problems. Great coaches work to make themselves dispensable—and therefore are never forgotten!

Appendix 1

Steps of Theater Inquiry

Disciplinary Inquiry is the process of

1. asking field-specific types of questions, and then
2. going about answering them in field-specific ways.

Each discipline and content area, by its very nature, asks certain types of questions and then uses an appropriate methodology to go about answering those questions. Therefore, both the question and the process must be appropriate to the specific field.

Focusing on inquiry (a field-appropriate question and methodology) allows students to act like experts within the field, use their creativity to see things from multiple perspectives and when they leave school, to have at their fingertips and habits of mind, multiple strategies to answer the questions they might confront in a rapidly changing world.

Basing units of instruction on inquiry allows for: sharing power in the classroom, provides for a naturally differentiated curriculum, allows students to make content learning more relevant, and allows students to contribute to the classroom using their strengths rather than focusing on their weaknesses.

The purpose of theater is "the expression of the human experience through representative actions" (Kolis, 2011). For our students that means to identify an important human experience—from their point of view right now—and learn how to best represent that experience.

When done well, theater can in fact enhance the quality of our students' lives because they have had the opportunity to examine that human experience from multiple perspectives and decided what was important enough to create representative actions.

Steps of Theater Inquiry

Step 1: Observation (experiences)—a sensory, rich, real-life (concrete) experience for the learner.

Our senses are the only ways by which information gets into our beings. Think about that for a moment—the only way you "know" something is to have seen it, heard it, tasted it, smelled it, felt it, or moved it

Combining concrete experiences with how individuals process those experiences is even more powerful in terms of learning. Not everyone thinks about their experiences in the same ways—they group them differently, they rank them, they connect them; they basically process those experiences in ways that make sense to themselves.

Step 2: Curiosity (ask questions) about what has been experienced.

Relevance makes the learning journey worthwhile. Things that we care about are worth our time, effort, and resources to "get" or achieve. (Think about one of your hobbies for a moment—do you not spend your time, effort, and some of your resources because you care about it—is it relevant to you?)

To wonder about something is the beginning of relevance. Unfortunately in schools, most kids learn that it does not pay to be curious because the teachers know all the right answers. That means you have to RE-teach students to wonder about how things work, how things are connected, why things occur the way they do, and so on.

Curiosity is grounded in creativity and that means lots of questions and lots of different perspectives and ways of combining things. Creativity is all about LOTS—of ideas, thoughts, different ways of doing things, different perspectives on the same idea.

Step 3: Problem statements (define the problem to be studied).

A point in every direction is the same as no point at all. Therefore, problem statements provide a direction. They say "Here is the one idea that I am going to focus on and this is what I am going to do about it." The word "problem" here does not mean "obstacle to overcome" but here is defined as: *a question raised for inquiry, consideration or solution* (*Merriam-Webster's Dictionary*).

Step 4: Gathering information

Future actions need to be based in solid content knowledge rather than only personal experiences. Solid content knowledge includes facts that the field has determined to be valid, reliable, the best course of action, what the field currently knows and is based upon multiple experiences and over a longer period of time. While personal experiences are important, field-specific and field-approved content has more validity, is more reliable, and is frequently more accurate.

Step 5: Create/construct
: How will we as performers represent that one specific human experience? What words, what actions, what context must we provide to share our perspectives? The audience will be real (when we perform) so everything does in fact matter!

Step 6: Review/test
: First draft done. We run through our first best attempt—and then using specific expert criteria, review our work.

Step 7: Revise
: Using those specific expert criteria, we revise our first attempt.

Step 8: Perform
: First for our classmates—then for real!!

Step 9: Analysis of the entire process
: Analysis here in the process is focused on student learning not just the DOING portion of the process. Analysis here acts as a *review of what the learner has done*; it is in fact a list.

Step 10: Conclusion—what have we learned?
: Reflection is the foundation of powerful learning. It says "I used to think like this, believe this, and was able to do these things. Now I think like this, believe this, and can do these skills." Therefore, reflection is based upon an individual's past context (what they thought they already knew) compared to their more current views.

  Note: Doing inquiry looks different discipline to discipline. Theater is both a *product* of inquiry and a *method* of inquiry, and it's easy to conflate the two, especially since we all have more experience with the products of theater (movies, YouTube videos, Shakespeare) than the process of theater. Inquiry is asking discipline-specific questions and answering them in discipline-specific ways. Theater is a way of proposing questions as well as answering them.

The Steps of Theater Inquiry should be enacted *by theatrical means to ask questions about theater.*

Appendix 2

SCAMPER

SCAMPER is a creativity strategy for modifying and developing more ideas from a list or idea you already have. It helps to trigger directions or ideas that haven't been considered before. SCAMPER is a mnemonic device where each letter stands for the following:

- S = Substitute: plug in one idea for another you already have; what might you use instead? What would work as well or better? The last unit I taught focused on "power (bullying)," I could substitute "relationships" for this next unit.
- C = Combine: put two or more ideas together; What might work well together?
- A = Adapt: change one idea that works someplace else to fit your needs; how could you make it fit? What could be changed to fit your purpose or condition?
- M = Modify, Minify, Maxify: make your idea or part of your idea bigger, smaller, fit better; What would happen if you changed it slightly—larger, smaller, greater, stronger, lighter, slower, and so on?
- P = Put to other uses: use your idea for something else; how could you use it for a different purpose? What are some new ideas to apply it?
- E = Eliminate: get rid of part of an idea; What could you do without? What could you subtract or take away?
- R = Reverse, rearrange: look at the idea from a different perspective, backwards, on top, sideways, switch pieces around; What would you have if you turned things around, change the order, parts, layout, sequence?

It is our belief that the lessons provided for you in section 3 can be easily modified to meet your needs whether you use SCAMPER or another creative strategy. The important thing to remember is that the lessons are a starting place for you. Use them as a launching-off point into a world where you and your students are truly doing theater!

Appendix 3

Getting the Most from Experiences

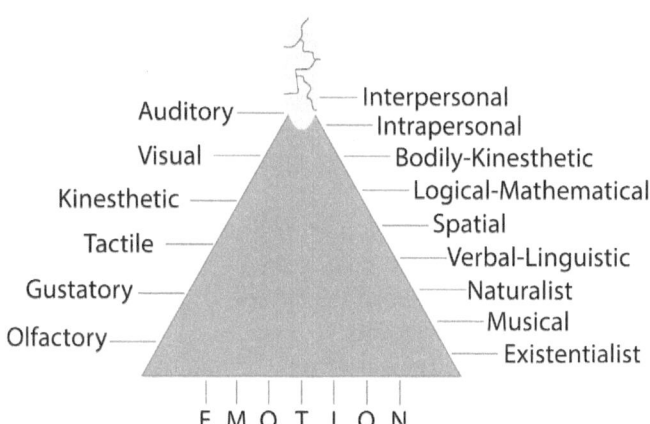

Diagram explanation:

One triangle represents one's experience with something. The "sticks" on the left side represent our senses—the ways we get information into our beings. Every individual uses some senses more than others (more is better in terms of information).

When we process information, we think about it in certain ways (the sticks on the right side) and connect the new experience to prior experiences.

For each experience, we use our senses (sticks on the left) and process that information in our own specific ways (sticks on the right). Every experience is also personalized by the lens of life (lens on the top) that an individual chooses (sometimes) to use for that experience.

The foundation for using experiences for learning rests upon the level of "emotion" of the experience. Things that are highly emotional (either good or bad) go right into our long-term memories.

Experiences start with our senses (at least for our public school–aged students). Our bodies have a natural three-dimensional inclination—we just like having 3D experiences. Watch a child "play" and you'll observe them using almost all of their senses. 3D means that an object has weight, heft, texture, smell, taste, sound, color, shape, and moves in certain ways. These types of 3D experiences are called "concrete" experiences and in terms of learning are the strongest and most personal.

1. Visual (sense of sight)—our sense of sight inputs data into our brains by translating light into images and colors. This includes color, lightness, darkness, form, depth, shape, and focus.
2. Auditory (sense of sound)—our sense of sound inputs data into our brains by translating perceived sound waves as electrical impulses. This includes pitch, rhythm, timbre, and volume.
3. Kinesthetic (sense of movement)—our sense of movement puts information into our brains such as pressure, balance, and movements. Kinesthetic here has a large muscle orientation. This includes walking, running, acting, jumping, and role-playing.
4. Tactile (sense of touch)—our sense of touch puts information into our brains such as pressure, heat, cold, pain, soft, hard, rough, and smooth. Touching objects is fundamental to learning, especially early on (thus the intrigue of children's museums).
5. Olfactory (sense of smell)—our sense of smell reaches directly into our emotions and memory (think of dirt or perfume). Frequently when we describe smells, we say, "This reminds me of (my grandmother's house, a trip, a boy/girlfriend/partner)."
6. Gustatory (sense of taste)—our sense of taste inputs data into our brains by translating taste into sweet, salty, bitter, and sour (closely related to smell). Very frequently, we compare tastes (tastes like chicken) which are culturally biased, because we have not developed a large vocabulary for describing tastes generally.

Note: For Sense Thinking Questions the key is to have students *describe what they observe* (not the conclusions they draw from what they see). For example if you give them a pencil and ask them to make observations about what they see, they will frequently say "pencil" rather than make observations such as "it is 5 inches long, it is yellow, it has 5 sides. ..."

We frequently do not have good language to describe our experiences (taste and smell are notoriously difficult). It appears so basic that we jump right to conclusions rather than the observations (think Sherlock Holmes). Jumping to conclusions is natural—knowing a pencil is a pencil is not wrong, just not the point of the exercise. The key for making observations is to learn to notice the unnoticed.

Processing our observations (sticks on the right side) means how we "think about" the information we took in (connections, relationships). We personalize the data we noticed (our senses) and since each person is an individual, we each emphasize some areas more than others do. Processing observations includes the relationships we create with and between experiences and also how we connect those new experiences to our prior experiences.

1. Interpersonal—this intelligence focuses on how we relate to others, your sensitivity to the moods, feelings, temperaments, and motivations of others, and your willingness to cooperate to work as a group of individuals. Interpersonal intelligence goes beyond noticing those things about others to "being swayed" by them when making decisions.
2. Intrapersonal—this intelligence stresses knowledge of self, the willingness and frequency of introspection, and the ability to self-reflect without those "rose-colored glasses." Intrapersonal intelligence includes knowledge about one's personal strengths and weaknesses, uniqueness, and the ability to predict one's own reactions and thoughts.
3. Bodily-kinesthetic—this intelligence includes the idea of being movement and touch driven. It includes the capacity to handle objects skillfully (making things), as well as dancing, acting, and sports. People who are bodily-kinesthetic intelligent communicate experiences and thoughts through movement, or creating objects that are meant to be felt.
4. Logical-mathematical—this intelligence includes a focus on relationships (between items, not necessarily between people). These relationships include ideas of logic, abstractions, reasoning, numbers, critical thinking, cause and effect, correlation, sequence, and predictions.
5. Spatial—this intelligence stresses the ability to create 2D and/or 3D representations. It focuses on the ability to visualize with the mind's eye, see things from a different perspective (top, bottom, side, above, etc.), and the ability to communicate experiences and thoughts through those 2D and/or 3D representations.
6. Verbal-linguistic—this intelligence focuses on words and languages, reading, writing, telling stories, vocabulary, definitions, and poetry. The key is to communicate experiences/thoughts through words.
7. Naturalist—this intelligence sees everything connected in a world-system. Included ideas are classification, categories, niches, relationships, and structure and function.

8. Musical—this intelligence involves sounds, rhythms, tones, pitch, and how you hear things. People strong in this intelligence communicate their experiences and/or thoughts through sounds (not words).
9. Existentialist—this intelligence focuses on deep meanings (of life, tragedies, etc.), philosophy, and spirituality. The focus here in on the biggest picture possible (not all the small details), how everything works together toward some sort of end-in-mind.

Each individual has his/her own MI strengths and weaknesses. We *prefer* some ways of processing our experiences more than others. Asking students to explicitly notice characteristics for each experience allows them to reinforce those preferred ways of thinks AND develop their areas of weakness.

The lens is the cumulative weight of all our previous experiences. As such, it occupies the lofty peak on our diagram. Every experience a student is currently having is subject to and colored by the experiences of their past (their lens), even as it changes or reinforces that lens.

We all use multiple lenses every day that we look through to interpret our daily experiences. We take in information from our senses and our processing only after being filtered through our lenses. That means that not only do we focus on some information more than others (senses), connect them (or not) with prior experiences (processes), they are also viewed (and sometimes distorted) by the lens we chose to use.

These mental models are not "good" or "bad" they just are—to live to our greatest potential requires us to be aware of the lenses we have. Peter Senge (1990) has said (one of my favorite quotes of all time) "[the] structures of which we are unaware hold us prisoner." Your mental model is one of these structures.

Our lenses in life ultimately reflect our deepest beliefs about the world, beliefs that are so deeply embedded in our lives they seem to be "common sense" (to us). They are the values we carry with us every day to every experience. It is how we perceive the world—what we value, what we care about, and how we think things work.

Powerful experiences are not just about how many experiences you have had, they also include the notion of "How emotionally laden is the experience?" In our diagram, emotion is the foundation. I like to imagine that strongly emotional experiences have an intense color and that less emotional experiences have less remarkable colors (deep red for a deeply angering experience, a pale red for mild irritation, transparent for neutral).

Imagine a box of marbles mostly filled with clear marbles. The clear marbles represent the mundane experiences that you may or may not remember, like driving to work or opening a door. Now imagine that there are several intensely colored marbles among the clear ones: These vibrantly colored marbles represent highly emotional experiences, the more emotional the experience, the more intense the color of the marble. Compared to the mundane clear marbles, the vibrant marbles stand out, just like how out of all the days I attended class I can remember that one time I called my second-grade teacher "Mom" with perfect clarity.

Experiences with unusually strong emotional content go right into long-term memory, no matter what lens, sensory detail, or processes are associated with it. Emotion is the gatekeeper to long-term memory (think of your most embarrassing moment—no matter how long ago chances are your face still gets red, you start to sweat … the physiological body response of that emotion goes right along with your experience for years afterwards).

Strong emotions are frequently connected to success, failure, embarrassment, achievement, recognition, belittlement, pride, getting caught doing something "wrong," errors, meeting goals, novelty, unexpectedness, surprise, cognitive dissonance (ideas that defy what they think they know), AHA moments, punishment, and can be either personal or social in nature.

In terms of positive, emotionally charged learning, success is the greatest motivator. Success on any task is the result of four components: (a) the task itself; (b) personal ability/aptitude for that task; (c) time, effort, and resources allocated by the individual to the task; and (d) luck (time, day, teacher, classmates, etc.). The one component that students control is point c—time, effort, and resources they commit to the learning task.

One reason we need to celebrate more (a strong emotion) is that recognizing learning success allows students to put that positive experience into long-term memory. Having experienced success before gives students "hope" that they can be successful again. The teacher can then use that prior experience to help students overcome doubt when success is questionable.

One last note about using emotion as a learning tool. Things that students see as "relevant" have the emotional component built into the experience! Relevance matters to students because they are developmental in nature, have a needs orientation, answer their stressors and concerns, and when done well answer their own questions (AHA moments).

Appendix 4

Cross the Line Prompts

Cross to the other side of the line ...

... if you like action movies.
... if you like romantic movies.
... if you like comedies.
... if you listen to music with violent lyrics.
... if most of the music you own and listen to contain explicit lyrics.
... if you've ever made fun of someone for how they dress.
... if you have ever gotten into a physical fight.
... if you feel comfortable walking away from a challenge to fight.
... if you have cried in the past 6 months.
... if you received at least two As in school last year.
... if you like to play sports.
... if you like to watch sports.
... if you play in an organized sports league.
... if you have more than 100/200/500 friends on Facebook.
... if you have a friend who is gay.
... if your parents would be okay with you coming out as gay.
... if you have siblings.
... if you fight physically with your siblings regularly.
... if you watch the NBA.
... if you watch the WNBA.
... if you know who won the Men's College Basketball Championship.
... if you know who won the Women's College Basketball Championship.
... if you believe all races are treated equally.
... if you believe there will always be poor people.
... if you believe world peace is possible.

… if you think America is the greatest country in the world.
… if you believe some people are just bad/evil.
… if you believe you should be allowed to wear whatever you want to school.
… if you feel our education system works well for you.
… if you think of yourself as intelligent.
… if you feel all teachers treat you fairly.
… if you would come to school if it were optional.
… if you think this school does enough to stop bullying.
… if you feel safe walking into school every day.
… if you feel safe in your neighborhood.
… if you think we shouldn't help people in other countries.
… if you think everyone should have the right to be an American citizen even if they weren't born here.

Appendix 5

Circle of Power and Respect (CPR)

"The Circle of Power and Respect" is a concept developed by Linda Crawford (2012) in her book *The Advisory Book: Building a Community of Learners Grades 5–9*. Chip Wood (2007) also talks about the importance of having activities like the Circle of Power and Respect in the classroom in his text, *Yardsticks: Children in the Classroom Ages 4–14*. A similar concept was created by Roxann Kriete (2002), which is mentioned in her book *The Morning Meeting*.

The reason for having the Circle of Power and Respect or The Morning Meeting is to create a safe and productive learning environment. These techniques integrated into the classroom help create a sense of community that may lead to an atmosphere that facilitates powerful learning.

The Circle of Power and Respect involves four steps:

1. They say their name and/or a greeting.
2. They answer a sharing prompt (may or may not be related to the daily learning task).
3. They share announcements and/or daily news.
4. There is some sort of an energizer or movement sometime during the lesson.

For example, at the beginning of the hour, the students would:

1. Say their name (yes, they do it every day).
2. Answer a prompt (what is your favorite movie of all time? If you were an atom, which one would you be?).
3. Ask if there are any announcements that the class needs to know (sports competition, tryouts, news of note, etc.).

4. Have a rock-paper-scissors competition for 2 minutes halfway through class.

The idea is that by sharing students might find some common bonds with students with whom they might not normally interact. Learning is a risk-filled activity—not having any type of relationship with others in the class makes that risk even larger. Failing in a safe environment is preferable to failing in a class where you feel that everyone is out to get you.

Time is of course the enemy, so a modification (SCAMPER, appendix 2) of CPR is provided below:

MONDAY MEETINGS

The purpose of the Monday meeting is to be intentional about building community in the classroom. This means giving students an opportunity to share and it also allows students to practice active listening.

There are several variations of Monday meetings. This is the format I like to use: On Monday, I present the thought or question and respond to it myself. I then give students the opportunity to think about it for 24 hours. I have found that if I ask for students to respond immediately the answers are not as thoughtful. The next day at the beginning of class I ask three or four students to respond to the question. This usually takes no longer than 2 minutes. I then repeat this process each day of the week until all have had an opportunity to share.

A couple of things to take note of: First, students should not be forced to share (although most do). Second, students need to be reminded that this is time to listen. No comments or questions are given during this time. Finally, it is important to make sure that the environment is a safe one for students to share.

Appendix 6

Sample Script

The scene takes place on a farm. Cow, Rooster, and Lamb are all just waking up for the day.

Cow: Good morning Rooster and Lamb!
Rooster: Ugh, is it morning already? What time is it?
Lamb: It's 7:00 a.m. Time for breakfast!
Cow: I think I'll have bacon for breakfast.
Rooster: Don't let Pig hear you say that.
Lamb: Rooster, what do you want for breakfast?
Rooster: Um, whatever is leftover in the trough from last night is fine with me.
Cow: Looks like there is some corn and stale bread.
Rooster: Bread?! Oo give me some of it! I love bread!
Lamb: Look over there! The farmer is coming with fresh fruit and a whole new bale of hay!
Cow: I call the apples!
Rooster: Not if I get there first!
Lamb: You guys are so exhausting!
End Scene

Appendix 7

Stage Directions

Downstage Left	Downstage Center	Downstage Right
Stage Left	Center Stage	Stage Right
Upstage Left	Upstage Center	Upstage Right

Appendix 8

Blocking Activity

Directors decide on three pieces of the blocking and actors decide on the remaining two. Remember:

1. *The blocking must be meaningful and believable!*
2. *Include both actors in all of the blocking.*
3. *Include both the action and where the action should take place (stage direction).*

Actor A and Actor B arrive at a local circus. The circus performers become ill and ask Actor A and Actor B to fill in and complete the performance for the audience.

ENTRANCE Blocking 1:
Blocking 2:
Blocking 3:
Blocking 4:
EXIT Blocking 5:

Appendix 9

Script Writing

Remember: You must always have an entrance and exit blocked into your script

Option 1: The blocking appears in parenthesis and the character's name is followed by a colon before a spoken line.

(Stage Blocking)
Character's Name: _____.
(Stage Blocking)
Character's Name: _____.
EXAMPLE:
(Sarah and Jane enter stage left and walk to center stage)
Sarah: Hey Jane, what are you up to today?
Jane: I'm going to the mall. I'll go ask my mom if you can come with me.
(Jane walks off stage right and returns moments later)
Jane: She said you can come!
Sarah: Awesome!
(Jane and Sarah run off stage left to exit)

Option 2: The blocking appears in parenthesis in the center of the page and the character's name is written above a spoken line.

(Stage Blocking)
Character's Name
_____

(Stage Blocking)
Character's Name
_____.

EXAMPLE:

(Sarah and Jane enter stage left and walk to center stage)
Sarah
Hey Jane, what are you up to today?
Jane
I'm going to the mall. I'll go ask my mom if you can come with me.
(Jane walks off stage right and returns moments later)
Jane
She said you can come!
Sarah
Awesome!
(Jane and Sarah run off stage left to exit)

Appendix 10
Set Rendering

Appendix 11

Scoring Guide

Performance skills: Performance demonstrates articulation and projection ___/20
Actors can be seen and action is intentional
Facial expressions match the mood of the character/story

Depth of understanding: Demonstrates relation to the essential question ___/10
Costumes are relevant to the character/story
Set design aids in the telling of the story

Engaging: Performance draws the audience in ___/5

Script: Performance has a clear storyline ___/5

Evidence of collaboration: Each student has an equitable role in performance/process ___/10

TOTAL ___/50

Appendix 12

Story Arc

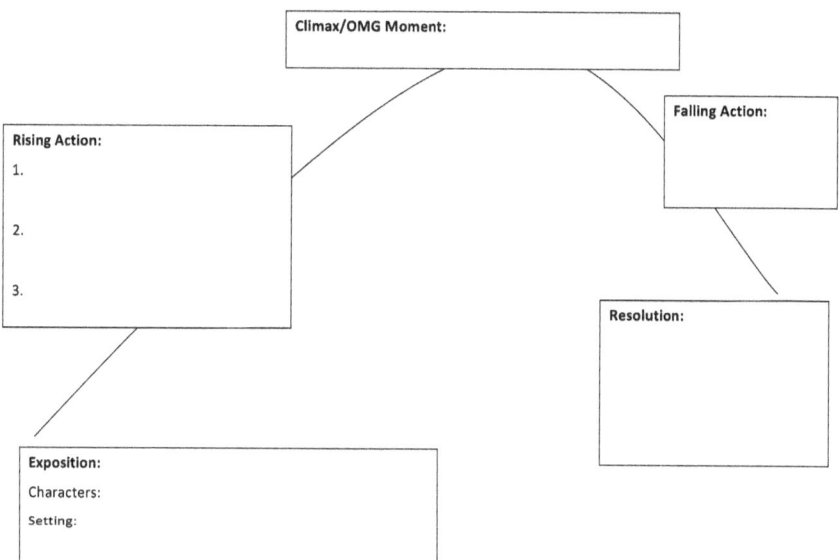

Appendix 13

Script Template

Remember: You must always have an entrance and exit blocked into your script.

Appendix 14

Feedback Form

Remember to be specific and use examples!

Positive:

Positive:

Positive:

Problem:

Solution:

Appendix 15

Costume Worksheet

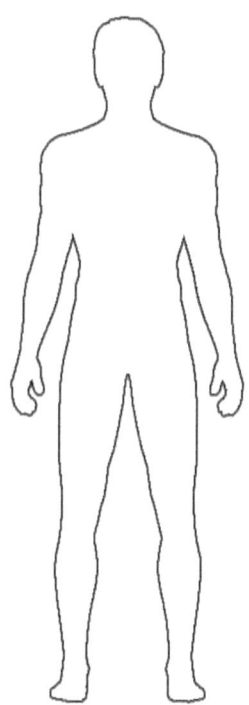

Appendix 16

Set Design Worksheet

Appendix 17

Set and Costume Planning Worksheet

1. What is your vision for the set (if you had to describe what the set would look like to someone who will never see it, what would you say?)? Include colors, materials used, and so on.

   _____
   _____
   _____
   _____
   _____
   _____
   _____

2. What is your vision for the costumes? Include colors, fabrics used, and so on.

   _____
   _____
   _____
   _____
   _____
   _____
   _____

3. Make a list of costume pieces you will need:

_____ _____
_____ _____
_____ _____
_____ _____
_____ _____
_____ _____

4. Make a list of set pieces/props you will need:

_____ _____
_____ _____
_____ _____
_____ _____
_____ _____

Appendix 18

Performance Reflection Worksheet

1. Something I can do now that I couldn't do before is...

   _____
   _____
   _____
   _____
   _____

2. If I were to do this again, I would...

   _____
   _____
   _____
   _____
   _____

4. Which character from your own scene did you relate to the most and why?

   _____
   _____
   _____
   _____
   _____

5. What connections did you make to other performances?

   _____
   _____
   _____
   _____
   _____

6. How did the blocking of your scene help to tell the story?

_____
_____
_____
_____
_____

7. How did the set and costumes of your scene help to tell the story?

_____
_____
_____
_____
_____

8. Fitting in means…_____

References

Block, P. (2008). *Community: The Structure of Belonging*. San Francisco, CA: Berrett-Koehler Publishing.

Bransford, J., Brown, A., & Cocking, R. (Editors). (2000). *How People Learn*. Washington, D.C.: National Academy Press.

Brown, J. & Moffett, C. (1999). *The Hero's Journey*. Alexandria, VA: ASCD.

Bybee, R. (2015). *The BSCS 5E Instructional Model—Creating Teachable Moments*. Arlington, VA: NSTA press.

Cervetti, G. & Tilson J. (2008). *Powerful Learning*. San Francisco, CA: Jossey-Bass.

Cool Runnings. Film. Directed by Jon Turteltaub. Burbank, CA: Walt Disney Home Video, 1999.

Covey, S. (1998). *The 7 Habits of Highly Effective Teens*. New York, NY: Simon & Schuster.

Crawford, L. (2012). *The Advisory Book*. Minneapolis, MN: Developmental Designs.

Darling-Hammond, L., Barron, B., Pearson, P., Schoenfeld, A., Stage, E., Zimmerman, T., Cervetti, G., & Tilson, J. (Editors). (2008). *Powerful Learning*. San Francisco, CA: Jossey-Bass.

DeNitto, J. & Strickland, J. (1987). Critical thinking: A skill for all seasons. *College Student Journal*, 21(2), 201–204.

Davis, G.A. (2004). *Creativity Is Forever* (5th ed.). Dubuque, IA: Kendall/Hunt.

Dewey, J. (1938). *Experience & Education*. New York, NY: Touchstone.

Eberle, B. (2008). *Scamper: Creative Games and Activities for Imagination Development*. Waco, TX: Prufrock Press.

Egolf, D.B. (2001). *Forming, Storming, Norming, Performing*. Lincoln, NE: Writers Club Press.

Glasser, W. (2001). *Choice Theory in the Classroom*. New York, NY: HarperPerennial.

Kolis, M. (2011). *Student Relevance Matters: Why Do I Have to Know This Stuff?* Lanham, MD: Rowman & Littlefield.

Kolis, M. (2013). *Rethinking Teaching*. Lanham, MD: Rowman & Littlefield.

Kolis, M. & Krusack, E. (2012). *Powerful Ideas in Teaching.* Lanham, MD: Rowman & Littlefield.

Kriete, R. (2002). *The Morning Meeting Book.* Turner Falls, MA: Northeast Foundation for Children.

Kubler-Ross, E. (1969). *On Death and Dying.* New York, NY: Touchstone.

Lencioni, P. (2002). *The Five Dysfunctions of a Team.* San Francisco, CA: Jossey-Bass.

Merriam-Webster's Collegiate Dictionary. Tenth Edition (2002). Springfield, MA: Merriam-Webster.

Miracle on Ice. Film. Directed by Gavin O'Connor. Burbank, CA: Buena Vista Home Entertainment, 2004.

Remember the Titans. Film. Directed by Jerry Bruckheimer. Burbank, CA: Walt Disney Home Video, 2001.

Schon, D.A. (1983). *The Reflective Practitioner: How Professionals Think in Action.* US: Basic Books.

Senge, P.M. (1990). *The Fifth Discipline.* New York, NY: Currency Doubleday.

The Mighty Ducks. Film. Directed by Stephen Herek. Burbank, CA: Walt Disney Home Video, 1992.

Tuckman, B.W. (1965). Developmental sequence in small groups. *Psychological Bulletin,* 65(6), 384–399.

Wood, C. (2007). *Yardsticks.* Turner Falls, MA: Northeast Foundation for Children.

www.ingramcontent.com/pod-product-compliance
Lightning Source LLC
Chambersburg PA
CBHW020739230426
43665CB00009B/495